This is a truly remarkable, page-turning book that is peppered with personal illustrations and persuasively and winsomely presents a robust defense of the baptism of infants of believers. Written from the overflow of the big heart that this pastor and father has for children and the church, it excels at being biblically enlightening, doctrinally sound, experientially balanced, and practically helpful. The Q&A section is superlative—so succinct, so wise, so "spot-on." One does not have to agree with every detail Jason Helopoulos propounds in order to realize that this book has immense potential to move the church community forward by helping it to grasp the beauty of baptism without either overestimating or underestimating it. Highly recommended!

—**Joel R. Beeke**, President, Puritan Reformed Theological Seminary

This is an immensely helpful study of God's Word on a very important topic. The Q&A at the end alone is worth the read. If you want to understand Reformed teaching on baptism, look no further.

—**Michael Horton**, J. Gresham Machen Professor of Systematic Theology and Apologetics, Westminster Seminary California

In this scripturally based, theologically sound, and practically helpful book, Jason Helopoulos has provided a concise yet robust resource for anyone who wants to know more about the truth and beauty of covenant baptism. As he rightly states in the first chapter, the key to understanding and embracing baptism is knowing "the kindness of our covenant-making God." In other words, God is so incredibly gracious that he lavishes amazing gifts on his people *and* their children. Baptism is one of those gifts. I will be recommending and using this book frequently.

—**Julius J. Kim**, President, The Gospel Coalition

Jason Helopolous, in this highly readable volume, has given us the theological foundation for why the sign and seal of the new covenant, baptism, is to be placed upon believers and their covenant children to affirm their faith in Christ, who fulfills his promises—including "I will be a God to you and to your children after you." An additional blessing of this volume is the consequential foundation it presents for parenting based upon the promises of God and the anticipation of the covenant blessings he will bring in and through families by his sovereign grace.

—**Harry L. Reeder III**, Senior Pastor, Briarwood Presbyterian Church, Birmingham

Discussions of baptism can so easily raise the temperature in the church and draw lines among Christians. We may be grateful to Jason Helopoulos for gifting the church with a clear, accessible, irenic, and practical treatment of the Bible's teaching on baptism. Whether you have been thinking about these questions for a long time or for the first time, *Covenantal Baptism* will inform your mind and stir your heart as Helopoulos shows you the blessing that God intends for baptism to be.

—**Guy Prentiss Waters**, James M. Baird Jr. Professor of New Testament, Reformed Theological Seminary

COVENANTAL
BAPTISM

BLESSINGS OF THE FAITH
A Series

Jason Helopoulos
Series Editor

Covenantal Baptism, by Jason Helopoulos
Expository Preaching, by David Strain
Persistent Prayer, by Guy M. Richard

COVENANTAL
BAPTISM

JASON HELOPOULOS

P U B L I S H I N G
P.O. BOX 817 • PHILLIPSBURG • NEW JERSEY 08865-0817

If you find this book helpful, consider writing a review online
—or contact P&R at editorial@prpbooks.com with your comments.
We'd love to hear from you.

Unless otherwise indicated, Scripture quotations are from the ESV® Bible (The Holy Bible, English Standard Version®), copyright © 2001 by Crossway, a publishing min-istry of Good News Publishers. Used by permission. All rights reserved.

The quotation marked KJV is from the King James Version of the Bible.

Italics within Scripture quotations indicate emphasis added.

Printed in the United States of America

Library of Congress Cataloging-in-Publication Data

Names: Helopoulos, Jason, author.
Title: Covenantal baptism / Jason Helopoulos.
Description: Phillipsburg, New Jersey : P&R Publishing, [2021] | Series:
  Blessings of the faith | Summary: "Informative and encouraging, this
  brief book serves as a primer and quick reference tool regarding
  Presbyterian baptism for pastors, elders, prospective new church
  members, parents, and family members of children"-- Provided by
  publisher.
Identifiers: LCCN 2021008272 | ISBN 9781629957272 (hardcover) | ISBN
  9781629957289 (epub) | ISBN 9781629957296 (mobi)
Subjects: LCSH: Baptism--Presbyterian Church. | Christian education of
  children. | Presbyterian Church--Doctrines.
Classification: LCC BX9189.B3 H45 2021 | DDC 265/.1--dc23
LC record available at https://lccn.loc.gov/2021008272

For my mother
No son has been more blessed

CONTENTS

FOREWORD

It has often been said—sometimes with a sense of humor and sometimes in annoyance—that Presbyterian and Reformed churches love to do things "decently and in order." I can understand both the humor and the frustration that lie behind that sentiment. We love our plans, our minutes, our courts, and our committees. Presbyterian and Reformed folks have been known to appoint committees just to oversee other committees (reminding me of the old *Onion* headline that announced "New Starbucks Opens in Rest Room of Existing Starbucks"). We like doing things so decently that we expect our church officers to know three things: the Bible, our confessions, and a book with *Order* in its title.

But before we shake our heads in disbelief at those uber-Reformed types (physician, heal thyself!), we should recall that before "decently and in order" was a Presbyterian predilection, it was a biblical command (see 1 Cor. 14:40). Paul's injunction for the church to be marked by propriety and decorum, to be well-ordered like troops drawn up in ranks, is a fitting conclusion to a portion of Scripture that deals with confusion regarding gender, confusion at the Lord's Table, confusion about spiritual gifts, confusion in the body of Christ, and confusion in public worship. "Decently and in order" sounds pretty good compared to the mess that prevailed in Corinth.

A typical knock on Presbyterian and Reformed Christians is that though supreme in head, they are deficient in heart. We are the emotionless stoics, the changeless wonders, God's frozen chosen. But such veiled insults would not have impressed the apostle Paul, for he knew that the opposite of order in the church is not free-flowing spontaneity; it is self-exalting chaos. God never favors confusion over peace (see 1 Cor. 14:33). He never pits theology against doxology or head against heart. David Garland put it memorably: "The Spirit of ardor is also the Spirit of order."[1]

When Jason Helopoulos approached me about writing a foreword for this series, I was happy to oblige—not only because Jason is one of my best friends (and we both root for the hapless Chicago Bears) but because these careful, balanced, and well-reasoned volumes will occupy an important place on the book stalls of Presbyterian and Reformed churches. We need short, accessible books written by thoughtful, seasoned pastors for regular members on the foundational elements of church life and ministry. That's what we need, and that's what this series delivers: wise answers to many of the church's most practical and pressing questions.

This series of books on Presbyterian and Reformed theology, worship, and polity is not a multivolume exploration of 1 Corinthians 14:40, but I am glad it is unapologetically written with Paul's command in mind. The reality is that every church will worship in some way, pray in some way, be led in some way, be structured in some way, and do baptism and the Lord's Supper in some way. Every church is living out some form of theology—even if that theology is based on pragmatism instead of biblical principles. Why wouldn't we want the life we share in the church to be shaped by the best exegetical, theological, and historical reflections? Why wouldn't we want to be thoughtful instead of thoughtless? Why wouldn't we want all things in the life we live together to be done decently and in good order? That's not the Presbyterian and Reformed way. That's God's way, and Presbyterian and Reformed Christians would do well not to forget it.

Kevin DeYoung
Senior Pastor, Christ Covenant Church
Matthews, North Carolina

Introduction

BEGINNING WITH THE RIGHT PERSPECTIVE

Baptism. Need I say more? Too often, it is best known as the church family "celebration" that causes conflict. This sacrament seems to be fertile soil for debate, disagreement, ridicule, and even mocking among fellow brothers and sisters in Christ. Yet baptism lies at the very heart of the charge that our Lord and Savior gave to the church in the Great Commission of Matthew 28:18–20, and it represents, as we shall see in these pages, the core of the Christian faith—the gospel. When we approach it as a source of conflict and controversy, we miss the blessing that is attached to this sacrament, as well, and the kindness God has shown his people—the family of Christ—by gifting it to them. I hope that this book, beyond anything else, will show you this blessing and kindness.

I take it for granted that if you are reading this book, you have some interest in the doctrine of baptism. That is good. That is right. Maybe you are a parent who is wrestling with whether you should baptize your child (or children). Maybe you are new to the Reformed tradition or wrestling anew with what you believe about baptism. Maybe you are a pastor attempting to articulate covenantal baptism more clearly, or a teenager wondering whether you should be "rebaptized" at the urging of friends, or a Christian parent wondering whether your wandering child's previous baptism means anything for him or her now. Maybe you are simply looking for a quick refresher on the reasons for and blessings of covenantal baptism. This book is written for you.

But before we enter the discussion on baptism, I ask you to make a commitment with me. John Rabbi Duncan, a Scottish Presbyterian from a former generation, once said, "I'm first a Christian, next a Catholic,[1] then a Calvinist, fourth a Paedobaptist,[2] and [finally] a Presbyterian."[3] He places the right things in the right order. Before you read further, commit with me in the tenor of Duncan's confession above, first, that you are a Christian; second, that you identify as a member of the universal church; and that everything else follows in importance.

We need to remain careful not to make too much of baptism on the one hand but neither to dismiss it with a nonchalant attitude on the other. Baptism is truly a "secondary doctrine." Yet it is a *significant* doctrine. Our beliefs regarding baptism inform our parenting, our expectations of our covenant children, and even what church we attend and join. And, since blessings are attached to this sacrament (as we shall see), we desire those blessings to be received by all who are able. Most of all, because baptism is a foundational part of the Christian faith, our view of it should be well-informed and biblical.

If those who practice covenantal baptism[4] by baptizing their children do so in contradiction to God's Word, then they put words (and especially promises) in the mouth of God that are untrue. And yet, if God counts children as members of the covenant community who are to receive this sign and seal of his covenant, then those who neglect covenantal baptism prevent covenant children from receiving one of God's chief means of grace for their lives and the life of the church. These practical and theological implications are why the "discussion" about baptism is not idle theological discourse.

It may be of some help for you to know that my own convictions went through a change regarding this subject. By God's grace and kindness, I came to saving faith in college. Faithful college-aged Christians shared the gospel with me, and I joined a ministry that emphasized the need for believers to be baptized as—and only as—believers.[5] When I went off to seminary for more biblical and theological training, the one thing "I knew that I knew" was that an individual must be a believing and confessing person of age in order to be baptized.

In fact, I remember sitting with my wife in a Presbyterian church on a sunny day in Dallas, Texas, and watching with horror as families brought their infant children forward for baptism. I recall the pastor holding one of these children in his arms. The child remained still and quiet—until the pastor applied the waters of baptism. As the water flowed, the child erupted; a piercing cry—one that it would be assumed only grown adult lungs could bring forth—echoed through the sanctuary. I turned to my wife and with a little too much glee whispered, "See— even that child knows it should not receive baptism!"

Years later, I now sit here typing as a Presbyterian pastor who finds covenantal baptism one of the greatest blessings our God has given us. Some who read this book will come to the same conclusion; others will not. Either way, our consciences must be informed and convinced by what we believe the Scriptures teach. I hope, through these pages, to provide at the very least a sound argument and a helpful discussion.

May the Lord be with you as you read, and may he encourage your soul with his ineffable kindness. I pray that you will see the blessing of the sacrament of baptism and the goodness our God has shown by gifting it to his people. Blessings upon your reading.

1

THE KINDNESS OF GOD

A family of six stands before their local church. It proves to be the odd Sunday on which the father chooses to wear his "Sunday best"—his normal Sunday-morning attire consists of a pair of pants and a short-sleeved shirt, but on this day he wears a coat and a tie. The mother of the family, adorned with a patterned dress, stands by his side. Three children, ranging from four to seven years old, gather around their parents' feet. Smaller hands are placed in larger hands, and one child, with curious eyes, searches the congregation for a friend. The mother's arms cradle a baby girl who is outfitted with a fine white dress. It glimmers as the early morning sunlight enters the sanctuary windows and falls on this infant child. The dress, a "baptismal gown," has belonged to the family for four generations, each of which has passed it down to the generation after them. Its history wonderfully represents the importance of this moment. This is a covenant family moment.

The parents beam with an air of pride, though anxiousness also seems to mark their faces. Who, besides the pastor, likes standing in front of a congregation? Most people who sit looking on from the pews know that this small child embodies answered prayer. Sadness has been an all too familiar companion to this couple over the past years. They would have stood as a family of seven, instead of six, this particular morning, but God's providence led to one of the greatest sorrows of their earthly lives. Yet they stand, a covenant family of God, beaming with great joy before their church family on God's day. Most importantly, they also stand before their covenant-keeping God.

In the moments that follow, their pastor provides an explanation of baptism, prays for their child, takes the little girl into his arms, and asks the parents a series of questions, as they reply with vows before God and before their brothers and sisters in Christ. The pastor then asks the congregation a question, and they respond by making a commitment to assist these parents in raising this covenant child. The scene is familiar to those who have occupied the pews of this little church over the decades. They know that their pastor radiates a particular joy on these mornings. He takes the child in his arms, dips his hand in the baptismal bowl, and, after saying the child's name, baptizes her in the "name of the Father, and the Son, and the Holy Spirit." In this way, this beautiful little girl receives the profoundly beautiful sign and seal of God's covenant promises: the waters of baptism. As is his habit, the pastor utters a short and simple yet strong prayer over the child before handing her back to her mother.

This is a very ordinary scene that uses very ordinary means—yet it is one that represents the very *extraordinary* grace of God. It is a covenantal moment, and it takes place in the midst of the covenant people of God.

As you read about this scene, you may find yourself either comfortable or uncomfortable with it. You may have watched a similar scene unfold dozens of times or may never have seen it before. Whatever your experiences, I hope that as we explore covenantal baptism together in this book, you will come to appreciate the gracious gift that God grants to his precious children— and to rejoice over it with thanksgiving.

But before we look at baptism directly, we first need to focus, in this chapter, on the kindness of God as it is seen through the covenants he enters into with his people. This provides us with the necessary framework for understanding the blessing of baptism itself.

The Starting Place: The Kindness of a Covenant-Making God

Fundamental to baptism is the kindness of our covenant-making God. That is the most important thing I want to impress on you in this book. Baptism is a gift from a kind Father who loves to lavish good things upon his children. As we will see, baptism serves as a sign and seal of the promises God makes to us in his covenant. He did not have to make a covenant, yet he did. He did not have to provide promises, yet he did. He did not have to give signs and seals to reassure us of his promises, yet he did. Kindness upon kindness. Therefore, before we venture into the specifics of baptism, let's turn to the beginnings of this covenant.

Covenants Defined

What is a covenant? The simplest definition is that it is a relationship that involves mutual commitments—albeit commitments that are not always equal to one another. In the Bible, we often see these commitments sealed in blood. O. Palmer Robertson describes a covenant as "a bond in blood sovereignly administered"[1]—a definition that is both concise and rich. Another modern theologian has defined a covenant as simply "an agreement between God and human beings, where God promises blessings if the conditions are kept or threatens curses if the conditions are broken."[2] When God enters into a covenant with another party, he makes a bond that includes a pledge of faithfulness. Those who keep the obligations of the covenant will receive blessing and life, while those who do not receive cursing and death.

Reformed theology maintains a bicovenantal (two-covenant) system.[3] God entered into a covenant with Adam, which is called the *covenant of works*. After the fall, God entered into a second covenant—what Reformed theologians have come to call the *covenant of grace*. The covenant of grace is an overarching covenant that threads itself throughout the pages of Scripture, making redemptive history one story of God's willing and working in this world.

The First Promise of the Gospel

We see the principal promise of the covenant of grace first being articulated in the garden, to Adam and Eve, in Genesis 3:15: a child will be born into this world who will crush the head of the serpent. This has been called the *protoevangelium*—the first gospel. As we continue through the Scriptures, we find that this same Promised One will also bring reconciliation between God and mankind. All the rest of the Scriptures, in both the Old and the New Testaments, unfold and realize the fulfillment of this great covenantal promise.

This covenantal promise greatly impacts the way we read and understand the Bible. It ties together the entire history of God's people and helps us to find continuity across the pages of Scripture.[4] From this covenantal view, we read the Bible as one book that tells one overarching story of promise about one Savior's coming to reconcile one people to the one true God.

The Promise Takes Shape

Although foreshadowed in Eden, God's covenant of grace is not formally inaugurated until the time of Abraham, when God revealed that the Promised One would be Abraham's descendent. "What was the Abrahamic covenant in the highest reaches of its meaning?" John Murray, a stalwart theologian of the early twentieth century, asked. "Undeniably and simply: 'I will be your God, and ye shall be my people' (*cf.* Gen. 17:7; Exod. 19:5, 6; Deut. 7:6; 14:2; Jer. 31:33). In a word it is union and communion with Jehovah, the God of Israel."[5] Paul, as he is writing to the Galatians, identifies the Abrahamic covenant with the gospel when he says, "And the Scripture, foreseeing that God would justify the Gentiles by faith, preached the gospel beforehand to Abraham, saying, 'In you shall all the nations be blessed'" (Gal. 3:8; see also Gen. 12:3). Through the Abrahamic covenant, the seed who would be born of the woman and who would crush the head of the serpent is now identified as being a seed of the line of Abraham.

The gracious promises contained in the Abrahamic covenant prove so significant that one could argue that the verses that refer to them[6] are, from a Reformed perspective, the most significant in all the Bible. "Everything that God has done since [the Abrahamic covenant] to the present moment he has done in order to fulfill his covenant to Abraham."[7] And truly, all the nations are blessed beyond blessed.

Abraham's Desire for a Sign

Let's take a look at this Abrahamic covenant. At the beginning of Genesis 15, a few chapters after God's initial promise to him, he tells Abraham,[8] "Fear not, . . . I am your shield; your reward shall be very great." But then this narrative of promise seems to be interrupted by doubt. Abraham, who is an elderly man at this point, hears this promise and doesn't hesitate to point out to God, in verse 2, "God, you promised to make me a great nation and to bless all the nations of the earth through me, but I'm childless still." Concerned, and even doubtful, Abraham asks a similar question in verse 8 about the land that God has promised he will possess: "How am I to know that I shall possess it?" The great father of the faith questions God. Does that unsettle you? Does it unsettle our God?

When we think of God, I hazard to guess that most of us imagine him holding to the old adage that many of our parents said over and over: "A child should be seen but not heard." *Abraham, keep your mouth closed!* we think. *God just spoke and made you a promise.* But God does not operate by such an adage. As we shall see, he responds to Abraham's question with tender, fatherly kindness.

Now, we can ask God inappropriate questions and speak to him in an inappropriate way. But I don't believe Abraham is doing that here. We are told in verse 6 that Abraham "believed the LORD." His question in verse 8 is one that seeks clarity. He asks, "How am I to know . . . ?" We see in Abraham's questions not unbelief or even frailty but a cry to be reassured. He possesses trust, but he longs for that trust to be strengthened. His faith seeks assurance—and faith that seeks assurance is not faithlessness.

In fact, Paul says of Abraham in Romans 4:18, "In hope he believed against hope, that he should become the father of many nations."

Imagine that it's Valentine's Day and a young wife wakes up early in the morning, leaps out of bed, and runs to the kitchen. She desires to see whether her husband has left something on the table before he went to work. Is she wrong to do so? No. Does she look with anticipation because she doubts his love? No. Yet she finds herself reassured of his love as she enters the kitchen and sees a dozen roses in a vase and a box of her favorite chocolate truffles on the breakfast table. When she reads the handwritten love note he has left, her trust in his love strengthens all the more. She didn't doubt his love for her; she simply sought to have it encouraged.

To look to God is to look rightly. In fact, we could even say that it is only faith that allows for questions such as Abraham's that are directed toward the God of our faith. Abraham is wrestling with his concerns—the child promised to him has yet to appear, and the land God promised he has yet to possess.

The heartache we see in Abraham here flows from his desire to be reassured of God's promise to bless the whole world through him. He is concerned not simply with the promised land or the promised descendants but with the *Promised One*—the seed of the woman, known as the Messiah, who would crush the head of the serpent once and for all.

God Makes a Covenant with Abraham

Our Father in heaven is "merciful and gracious, slow to anger, and abounding in steadfast love and faithfulness" (Ex. 34:6). His tender, fatherly kindness is on display as he meets Abraham's questions. Our covenant-keeping God reassures Abraham in the most demonstrative of ways: by entering into a formal covenant with him. It is frankly astounding that the sovereign God of the universe would do this.

The act of making a covenant, which was well known in the ancient world, involved separating animals in half. The two parties who were involved in the covenant then walked through the path that lay between the separated halves of the animals. As they traversed that path, they pledged blessing to each other if they kept the covenant—but also vowed that if one of the parties transgressed their promise to the other, then they were to be divided as the animals had been. There was either blessing or curse—depending on the parties' faithfulness to the covenant. Here is "a bond in blood."

As I said, this covenant event is not strange to Abraham. But then it becomes quite strange. God puts Abraham into a deep sleep. A smoking torch, which foreshadows the pillar of clouds and fire that will lead Israel through the wilderness and will appear on Mount Sinai, alone passes through the severed pieces. This is unique! We possess no ancient Near Eastern documents that show a king making a self-maledictory oath and calling down curses upon himself as he gives covenantal promises to one of his subjects. As the only party to pass between the divided animals, God alone promises to take the punishment if either party breaks the covenant. And, in his eternal infinite knowledge and according to his divine decree, he knows that his covenantal pledge to bless Abraham and the nations will lead to the crucifixion of the very Son of God in the flesh.

This should astound us. God has no need to enter into a covenant with Abraham. He has already promised him—and God's word is trustworthy. "God is not man, that he should lie, or a son of man, that he should change his mind" (Num. 23:19). Then why does he make this covenant with Abraham? The answer should make our souls leap with joy. He enters into this covenant to reassure him. By cutting this covenant, he says to Abraham, "I want your faith to be as solid as possible." And this action of reassurance will cost our God severely.

At the very beginning of this passage, before Abraham asked a single question, God said, "Fear not, . . . I am your shield; your reward shall be very great." Now God shows Abraham—and us—what it means that he is a shield, and we see that he is in fact our great reward. He will prop up Abraham's faith on every side. It is truly astounding. God enters into covenant with a fallen man! You and I have not even begun to comprehend the steadfast love and kindness of our God. We will have all of eternity to contemplate this, and still we won't even begin to fathom its depths.

The Sacrament of Circumcision

When we turn in our Bibles from Genesis 15 to Genesis 16, we find that Abraham and Sarah still have no children, though they are even older. Sarah, in an act of unbelief and desperation, appeals to Abraham to take her female servant Hagar as a concubine. When waiting on God proves difficult, the machinations of men always allure—Abraham follows the advice of his wife, and Hagar conceives a child. But here is the kicker: this child is not the promised son who will come. God will not work according to our strategies or timetables. Our plans can never supplant his own.

I understand Abraham and Sarah's frustration. I even understand their desperation. And yet I expect God not to. As I read this account, I'm prepared for God to strongly rebuke Abraham and Sarah: "Not only do you have my word, but I have sealed it with an oath in blood! How dare you act in unbelief!" But that is not what we find. Instead, in Genesis 17, we witness the kindness of our God yet again. God meets Abraham in his weakness. He gives Abraham a sacrament to serve as a "sign" and "seal" of their covenant—namely, circumcision (Rom. 4:11).

> This is my covenant, which you shall keep, between me and you and your offspring after you: Every male among you shall be circumcised. You shall be circumcised in

the flesh of your foreskins, and it shall be a sign of the covenant between me and you. (Gen. 17:10–11)

God had given Abraham a promise—and his word had been sufficient. Yet he had also formalized it by making a covenant—and now, as Abraham's faith still wavers, he grants him a tangible, physical sign through the sacrament of circumcision that is to be applied to every male who belongs to the covenant people of God. Here is a sign of this covenant that Abraham and his male children would bear in their flesh for generation after generation. Astounding kindness!

God's Kindness Shown in the Sacraments

The gift of circumcision is a sacrament—a "visible sign of invisible grace."[9] Augustine, the great fourth-century theologian, helpfully explained that sacraments are God's Word made visible; they take what we *hear* and help us to *see* it. What God promised by his word, they now demonstrate in ways that we can see and feel. And that is a sheer act of kindness. There is no need for God to supplement his promises—he is trustworthy and cannot lie. Yet he provides signs of his covenant promises time and time again: the tree of life, and the tree of the knowledge of good and evil, to Adam; the rainbow to Noah; circumcision, here, to Abraham; the Passover to Israel; the Sabbath to the nation at the foot of Mount

Sinai; and baptism and the Lord's Table to the New Testament church.

God grants these tangible, physical signs and seals to engage our senses and reassure our faith. John Calvin has said it better than any: "As our faith is slight and feeble unless it be propped on all sides and sustained by every means, it trembles, wavers, totters, and at last gives way. Here our merciful Lord, according to his infinite kindness, so tempers himself to our capacity that, since we are creatures who always creep on the ground, cleave to the flesh, and, do not think about or even conceive of anything spiritual, he condescends to lead us to himself even by these earthly elements, and to set before us in the flesh a mirror of spiritual blessings."[10] Our God knows that we exist as physical beings and that, as physical beings, we gravitate toward the visible. In fact, we desire not only to see but to touch, feel, smell, and even taste. His promise spoken to us should prove enough. Yet, like Abraham's, our faith remains weak. Like the father of the boy in Mark 9, all disciples of Christ can say, "I believe; help my unbelief." Through the sacraments, God meets us in our weakness and says, "I will keep, and I have kept, my promises." What kindness!

One of my great fears is that, when we discuss the sacraments, we miss the "heart" God has shown by gifting these blessings to us. God's greatness amazes us, and it should. But his greatness in and of itself does little to draw our hearts. It is the greatness of God married to the kindness of God that powerfully allures the human heart. And God's kindness radiates through this gift of the sacraments. As we reflect on the beauty of his kindness, these sacraments shine all the more brilliantly.

Sacraments as Signs

When it comes to the sacrament of circumcision, it is important for us to note that it served not primarily as a sign of family, racial, or national identity—although it did distinguish the Jews from the people of other nations—but rather as a sign and seal of the most extravagant spiritual blessings that God bestows upon man.[11] It served as a sign of our need to be cut off from the first Adam, of the corruption of our nature, and of God's provision for our fallenness. It signified our need to be regenerated and born again: "Circumcise yourselves to the LORD; remove the foreskin of your hearts" (Jer. 4:4). Paul points out in Romans 2:28–29 that "no one is a Jew who is merely one outwardly, nor is circumcision outward and physical. But a Jew is one inwardly, and circumcision is a matter of the heart, by the Spirit, not by the letter."

Notice that the sign of circumcision was applied to the male organ of reproduction. That is not accidental. Adam brought sin into the world, and "all mankind, descending from him, by ordinary generation, sinned in him, and fell with him, in his first transgression," as the Westminster Shorter Catechism states.[12] The sign of circumcision also signified God's covenant promise that he would send forth a Messiah, a Redeemer—the seed of the woman, a child of Abraham, a descendent of David—to be born into this world. God reminded sinners, through their own personal corrupted flesh, that even though mankind was fallen, he had promised to save his own through One who would be born. Every Jewish male bore this sign in the flesh as a continual reminder of God's covenantal promises that would come about through the seed of the woman.

When we turn to the New Testament, we no longer find circumcision being mandated. Why? Because it has been fulfilled. Paul tells us in Colossians 2:11 that Christ was circumcised through his crucifixion. Christ experienced the curse that we saw God committing himself to when he made his covenant with Abraham in Genesis 15. His crucifixion caused him to be circumcised because he was "cut off"—not merely from the flesh of his foreskin but from life itself. He received the judgment of God for us. Thus, the sign of circumcision no longer applies within the covenant community—it has been fulfilled. Yet God graciously continues to prop up our faith, so Christ gifted the sacrament of baptism as a sign of the promises of God.

As we said previously, there is one overarching covenant that stands over all redemptive history: the covenant of grace. However, because of the birth, death, resurrection, and ascension of Christ, we can speak about two general periods in the life of the covenant people of God:

the old covenant, before Christ, and the new covenant that follows Christ. As the sacrament of circumcision signified the promises of God to a person who entered into the covenant community in the old covenant, so baptism is the sacrament of initiation that signifies the promises of God to individuals who are under the new covenant. Both circumcision and baptism symbolize the need to be cut off from the first Adam and from the flesh as well as for cleansing, for being covered in blood, and for the hearts of God's people to be made new by the pouring out of the Holy Spirit. They are outward signs meant to denote an inward reality. Baptism, like circumcision, distinguishes the people of God from the world. It represents communion with God, identification with Christ, engagement in serving him and bearing his name. What was found in seed form in circumcision flowers in baptism. But now the sacrament of initiation into the covenant people of God is bloodless, because the blood has been already shed. Circumcision pointed forward to Christ who would be crucified; baptism points back to Christ already crucified.

Sacraments as Seals

As we consider the sacraments, we see as well that they are more than signs. Paul says in Romans 4:11 that circumcision also served as a seal. In ancient times, if I were to send a letter to a friend across the Mediterranean, I would write a message on a scroll and roll it up. And off it would go via courier. But how would my friend know that the letter, once delivered, had actually come from me? Well, I would melt some wax on the outside to keep the scroll bound tight. Then I would take my signet ring and seal the wax with my personal stamp. The parchment would then possess my seal—my imprimatur.

Paul points out that Abraham's circumcision sealed unto him the righteousness that was already his by faith. It impressed upon him the fact that he was indeed God's and that the promises of God, which he had received by faith, were his. As the Dutch theologian Bavinck summarized, "Seals . . . are distinguished from signs by the fact that they do not just bring the invisible matter to mind but also validate and confirm it."[13] Notice the language that Paul uses in that verse from Romans: he says that circumcision was "a seal of the righteousness that [Abraham] had by faith while he was still uncircumcised." That wording is important. Circumcision was not a seal of Abraham's subjective expression of faith. It was not a seal of his response to the gospel. Rather, circumcision functioned as a seal of the righteousness that he *received* from God through faith.[14] This means that the sacrament was not first about Abraham but about God. It was not first about what Abraham had or had not done but about what God had promised and done for him.

In the same way, baptism seals the promises of God to us. God uses it to impress upon our souls that each of us is in fact his. My baptism helps me to grasp not just that Christ died for sinners generally but that he died for me—a sinner. The grace of God is as real as the waters of baptism. Just as I was washed with the water, so I was washed with the blood of Christ. Even as I experienced baptism, so I truly experienced dying and being raised with Christ. All these things are impressed upon my mind, my soul, and my heart—sealed there. And, as was the case with Abraham and circumcision, baptism is not first about me or you but about him. It is not first about what you or I have done but about what he has promised and done for us in Christ.

Conclusion

It is easy for us to abstract the sacraments from their connection with the covenant of God. But when we do so, we abstract the sacraments from the God of the covenant. The great tragedy that results is a lost vision of who our God is. When we begin to see the sacraments as being first and foremost signs and seals of his covenant promises, the kindness of God appropriately thunders in our ears, shines before our souls, and grips our hearts. Our gracious and good heavenly Father provides these signs and seals to bless us and encourage us in the faith. Truly there is none like him. We couldn't even imagine or dream of a god who exercises his sovereign power toward his people more kindly than our covenant-keeping God does!

Questions for Further Reflection

1. How would you articulate the overarching story of the Scriptures? How does this story impact your reading and understanding of the Bible?

2. What are covenants? What was the purpose of the covenant God made with Abraham?

3. How are the sacraments related to the covenant? What do they primarily signify?

4. When you have found yourself discussing baptism with others, what have been the main themes of the conversations you have had with them?

5. Why do we often miss the kindness God has shown by gifting the sacraments to his people?

2

THE FOURFOLD STREAM
OF TESTIMONY

When many people discuss covenantal baptism, they assume that the wrong question needs to be answered: "Don't you believe in believer's baptism?" When someone asks me this, I answer, "Wholeheartedly!" But this is the wrong question. It is wrong because it fails to distinguish between a covenantal baptist view and a "believers *only*" baptist view. Everyone believes in "believer's baptism." If someone comes to saving faith in Christ as an adult and has not yet received the sacrament of baptism, either because they grew up outside the church or because the church of their youth didn't practice covenantal baptism, all Christian traditions agree that they should receive the sacrament upon professing their faith and entering into the membership of the covenant people of God. The real question that lies at the center of the debate over baptism is "Are children of Christian parents members of the covenant community—and therefore *also* right recipients of the sacrament of baptism?"

The Reformed tradition's answer to this question comes together from four streams of testimony: the testimony of covenantal continuity, of the New Testament Scriptures, of theology, and of the church.

The Testimony of Covenantal Continuity

As we attempt to understand what the Bible teaches about our children's eligibility for baptism, we desire to lean upon the whole counsel of the Scriptures (see Acts 20:27). And, as we saw in the last chapter, the covenant of grace is an overarching covenant that stands over the entire Bible. This has great implications for how we apply the sacrament of baptism.

From the very beginning, Reformed theology has drawn on the covenant to argue for infant baptism.[1] Why? Because God is a covenant-keeping God. He chooses to work, administer his grace, and enter into relationship with man by means of a covenant. The Bible records the progressive unfolding of God's covenant, which covers all of human history and provides unity across the pages of Scripture and throughout every period. As shown in the graphic below, if one covenant overarches both the Old and New Testaments, the primary result is continuity.[2]

We see that children were included and counted among the people of God under the old covenant, and God never repeals their inclusion under the new covenant. Old Testament children received the sign of their inclusion—circumcision—and therefore children are to receive the sign of inclusion that applies now in the New Testament period: baptism. Circumcision and baptism each serve as the rite of initiation for their respective times.

Covenant of Grace

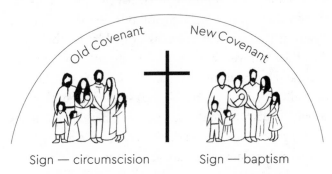

Sign — circumscision   Sign — baptism

An understanding of covenant continuity also offers an answer when people protest that the New Testament does not contain any mentions of child baptism. They desire proof. I would humbly contend, however, that the burden of proof falls on the baptistic side. The fundamental question regarding children's eligibility for baptism is whether they continue to be members of the covenant community. All believers recognize that children were regarded as members of this community from the time the covenant first began, with Abraham. If it is no longer the case that they are included in the covenant, this would indicate a monumental change in redemptive history and the way that God has chosen to work. If such a change had occurred, the proof of it would need to be clear.

But the baptistic view can offer no evidence for this exclusivist position. No example exists in the New Testament of a child being born and raised in a Christian home and then postponing their baptism until they are an adult. Proof for the baptistic position doesn't exist. Again, if the covenantal status of children—the status that they enjoyed among the people of God for two thousand years, from Abraham to the time of Christ—radically changed in the New Testament age, then we should expect to find the case for this change being clearly presented. But we don't. "How could a converted Jew regard the new covenant as a better covenant, if now his children were to be excluded from God's dealings with his people, no longer receiving a sign of God's covenant promises? If such were the case, Peter and later Paul would surely have had to face that question repeatedly. And yet it is never debated or even mentioned in the New Testament."[3]

If the advent of the New Testament era excluded children from the covenant community, a shadow would have hung over the good news that was being proclaimed. Children, who had always been part of the covenant community, would have been functionally excluded from that same community in a single epochal moment. Not only would this have been an issue that Peter and Paul would have had to address regularly, but it would have reigned in the mind of every Jewish parent who was entertaining the choice of embracing Christ.

New Testament Testimony

When we turn to the New Testament, we find additional support for the idea that children remain members of the covenant community.

Peter's Sermon at Pentecost

In Acts 2:38–39, we see Peter on the day of Pentecost urging his listeners, "Repent and be baptized every one of you in the name of Jesus Christ for the forgiveness of your sins, and you will receive the gift of the Holy Spirit." He continues by proclaiming, "*The promise is for you and for your children.*" We rightly consider Pentecost to be when the new covenant era was formally inaugurated with the outpouring of the Holy Spirit. And on this momentous occasion, Peter doesn't distance children from being included in the covenant community. Instead, he echoes an old promise.

Peter's words were falling on Jewish ears, and their meaning would not have been lost. He was echoing Genesis 17:7—a text that every self-respecting Jew would have known—in which God promises, "I will establish my covenant between me and you and your offspring after you throughout their generations for an everlasting covenant, to be God to you and to your offspring after you." Peter was asserting that the covenant promises of God extended to children in the new covenant era just as they had in the previous era.

Geoffrey Bromiley, a prominent twentieth-century theologian, noted the emphasis that Peter placed on the fact that the promise extended to those who were "far off, everyone whom the Lord our God calls to himself" (Acts 2:39). How strange it would be, then, for God to give "with one hand, extending the covenant in space, only to take away with the other, contracting the covenant in time."[4] He does not repeal the entire family's inclusion in the covenant—rather, through Peter, he emphasizes it! Children are still considered part of the covenant community.

Paul's Comparison of Circumcision with Baptism

Colossians 2:11–12 is a crucial passage for the discussion on baptism. In it, Paul clearly identifies circumcision with baptism. Each of them is an outward sign that is connected with a spiritual and inward reality: circumcision of the heart. Paul does not present one of the two as being more spiritual than the other. He says that we were circumcised in Christ when we laid aside the body of the flesh—that by faith we received a circumcision made "without hands." He is referencing the circumcision of the heart that is involved in our union with Christ. That circumcision of the heart is possible only because of the "circumcision" that Christ himself experienced upon the tree.

Paul then states that, just as we were circumcised in Christ, we were also buried with him in baptism. John Calvin, the magisterial Reformer of Geneva, comments, "What do these words mean, except that the fulfillment and truth of baptism are also the truth and fulfillment of circumcision, since they signify the one and the same thing? For he is striving to demonstrate that baptism is for the Christians what circumcision previously was for the Jews."[5] Paul teaches that both sacraments serve as signs of Christ's death, burial, and resurrection—circumcision looking forward to Christ's death and baptism looking back to it. If baptism and circumcision are thus equated, then baptism is logically to be applied to infants just as circumcision is.

Paul's Letters to the Ephesians and Colossians

Additional help with identifying whether believers' children are included in or excluded from the covenant is found in Ephesians and Colossians. Paul begins both letters by addressing them to "the saints" (Eph. 1:1; Col. 1:2). And, at the end of both letters, he includes children among those he is addressing by speaking to them in what have come to be called the "household passages" (see Eph. 6:1–4; Col. 3:20–21). Paul considered children to be members of the covenant community—that is why he addresses them specifically and even calls them "saints"! This means he is calling them "set apart"—not offering a commentary on their salvation but rather noting their unique position of belonging to the covenant community.

Furthermore, Paul admonishes children to obey their parents "in the Lord" (Eph. 6:1), because "this pleases the Lord" (Col. 3:20). Paul is exhorting them just as he exhorts the husbands, wives, slaves, and masters within the church. All of them are considered saints and directed to live, whatever their stations, to the honor of God. These children were fully embraced within the covenant community—and "if children were thus recognized and received in the apostolic churches, they were recognized as possessing the status of which baptism is the sign and seal."[6] It would be an odd thing, especially for a gospel people, if children were included right alongside husbands, wives, and masters under the requirements of the covenant community but excluded from the blessings of that same community. If they were included in it enough to receive its instructions, then surely they were included in it enough to receive its sign of belonging.

Paul's Writing on the Children of Believers

Paul makes clear the status that believers' children hold in relation to the covenant elsewhere in the New Testament as well. In 1 Corinthians 7:14, he describes children who have at least one believing parent as being "holy." He declares such a child holy based on even a single parent's faith and trust in the Lord. As he does in the above passages, Paul makes no comment on the children's subjective inward holiness but rather refers to their objective holiness. That is, Paul considers the children to be holy, or "set apart," because through their parents they belong to the covenant community and take part in its blessings and privileges. Christian children are unlike all the other children of the world. Their parents seek to raise them in the teachings of Christ; they enjoy privileges and blessings that a child who is raised in an unbelieving home does not enjoy (we will discuss this more in chapter 3). To baptize the children of believers is to recognize that they are distinct and set apart from the world.

Jesus and the Children

In Luke 18, Jesus has been speaking about the kingdom of God, and parents respond to his message by bringing their children to him in verse 15 so that he might bless them. The disciples, with much zeal and little understanding, attempt to keep the children away. Surely Jesus doesn't have time for children; he must busy himself with more significant people and minister to adults. But Jesus rebukes them. Mark, in his parallel account, says that Jesus is "indignant" as he does so (Mark 10:14). He isn't annoyed; he isn't slightly bothered—he is incensed that the disciples have come to such a conclusion and have tried to exclude children from his presence and blessing. He demands, "Let the children come to me; do not hinder them, for to such belongs the kingdom of God" (Mark 10:14). He does not say that the kingdom of God belongs to such that are *like* these—it belongs to these covenant children themselves.

Mark as well as Matthew close each of their parallel accounts of this passage with a description of Jesus laying his hands on the children and blessing them (see Matt. 19:15; Mark 10:16). Robert Reymond, a modern-day Reformed theologian, says concerning this, "Now Jesus' blessing, surely verbal and audible, was hardly comprehended by these infants and children, but this absence of comprehension on their part in no way nullified either the fact of the blessing itself on his part or the reality of their covenantal inclusion in the kingdom of God."[7] Christ blessed these children and considered them part of the covenant community; and though they may not have possessed the ability to recognize this blessing or the fact that they belonged, they nonetheless received the blessing and were regarded as belonging.

If Christ willingly blessed children during his earthly ministry, why would he change his ministry of blessing after he ascended? Not only does he remain the same Christ, but surely the blessing he offers from above is no less full than it was on earth. Baptism communicates the blessings that Christ gives to children, as well as his promises for them.

Household Baptisms
Household baptisms are mentioned in Acts 16:15 and 33–34, as well as in 1 Corinthians 1:16 (and possibly

also in Acts 10:47–48, in light of what Acts 11:14 says). Twelve instances of baptism are recorded in the New Testament[8] (though the church must have experienced a great number of them)—and fully one fourth of these recorded instances describe household baptisms. This proves consistent with the continuity we have been describing. Under the old covenant, God made a promise to Abraham that included his "household." Under the new covenant, God's promise continues to extend to the households of believers.

If a quarter of all the baptisms that the New Testament records involved entire households, and if the early church must have experienced a myriad of baptisms beyond these, it seems unlikely that none of the households that were baptized contained children. At the very least, there is no indication that children were excluded.

Theological Testimony

When we consider the overall systematic theology of the Scriptures, we find additional support for the idea that children continue to be members of the covenant community.

Family in Scripture

Throughout the Bible, God places an emphasis on the nuclear family. In fact, he chooses to work through the means of the family and ordained the family as the first societal institution. Therefore it comes as no surprise that this emphasis on the family characterizes the different covenants that God enters into throughout Scripture. He establishes his covenant with Noah as well as his family. In fact, the flood itself contained an element of "baptism" that involved both Noah and his entire family, since they were saved through the baptismal flood (see Gen. 7:1; Heb. 11:7).

As we saw in the first chapter, God also "cut" a covenant with both Abraham and his seed (offspring)—when he chooses to bless a patriarch, he includes their family in the blessing (see Gen. 17:12–13; 48:5–6). We see this emphasis upon family under the Mosaic covenant as well—in Deuteronomy 6 (as well as Psalm 78 and many other passages throughout the Scriptures), we see that God charges believing parents to bring their children up in the Lord. Joshua also speaks for his entire home when he declares, "As for me and my house, we will serve the Lord" (Josh. 24:15). The promises that God makes to David flow through his family (see 2 Sam. 7:12–17; Ps. 110). And these examples provide but a small sampling of this emphasis on family that we see throughout Scripture.

God has chosen, from the beginning, to work and extend his grace through families. This approach remains true throughout the Scriptures—we see it everywhere from Noah to the households that are described in Acts to the instructions that Paul's epistles offer to members of households (see Eph. 5:22–6:9; Col. 3:18–4:1). God chooses to work through the institution of the family as one generation passes on the faith to the next. The baptism of covenantal children, as circumcision did in the previous age, represents and clearly signifies this reality.

The Corporate Nature of Our Faith

The assertion that there are no grandchildren in the body of Christ is absolutely true, because no one receives salvation by virtue of their parents—each individual must possess faith themselves, and we all enter the narrow gate one by one. And yet, when we are saved unto Christ, we are also always saved unto the *body* of Christ (see Rom. 12:3–8; 1 Cor. 12:12–31; Eph. 4:1–16). The Christian faith cannot be understood apart from its corporate nature. This remains the consistent testimony of the Scriptures from the opening pages to the end (see Gal. 3:26–29; Eph. 2:11–22). And the sacrament of baptism reflects this truth. All the scenes of baptism in the New Testament, except for the account of the Ethiopian eunuch, portray multiple baptisms. Baptism was not, in those accounts, and is not, for us today, *simply* about the individual and Jesus—while it includes that element, there is more to it. There is a corporate nature to our faith, and covenantal baptism exemplifies it by marking children who are born into a covenant family with the baptismal sign of their entrance into the greater covenant community as well. They are children of their parents, but they are also children of the covenant—and God is calling them to believe in the Christ of the covenant community.

The Theological Focus

Baptism primarily testifies to what *God* promised to us and what *he* has secured for us (see Gal. 2:15–16; Eph. 2:8–10). Yet the baptistic view, although not always, tends to place its focus on *man* and his conscious decision. Bromiley states emphatically, if hyperbolically, that the baptistic view "gives the primacy and honor to humans and their work. . . . It finds the critical point in our turning to God rather than God's turning to us and God's work in turning us to God."[9] Personally, I find that the baptism of a small child pictures the helplessness of man (see Matt. 11:28–30), and his desperate need for God (see Rom. 8:1–8), better than almost any scene that we witness in the church. It testifies to all who are watching that only an act of God can save the small child being baptized.

Testimony of the Church

While we want our convictions to come from Scripture, we also cannot ignore the testimony that the church has offered throughout the ages—and covenantal baptism has been the church's historic practice. Early church fathers, including Origen, Cyprian, Tertullian, Hippolytus of Rome, and Irenaeus, all mention the baptism of infants during the second and third centuries.[10] Origen argued that, "according to the observance of the Church," baptism was to "also be given to infants; since, certainly, if there were nothing in infants that ought to pertain to forgiveness and indulgence, then the grace of baptism would appear superfluous."[11] The Council of Carthage, in AD 253, took infant baptism for granted. No one is able to point to a time when the practice began—Augustine, who understood baptism to be the New Testament counterpart of the Old Testament's sign of circumcision,[12] asserted in the fourth century that infant baptism had existed in the church for as long as anyone could remember.[13] The historical record indicates that the church always practiced covenantal baptism. Until the time of the Anabaptists in the sixteenth century, we witness no noticeable outcry against the practice of baptizing children in the church. And the majority of the church universal today—not to mention the overwhelming majority of people who have made up the church throughout the centuries—holds to an infant baptism position.

Conclusion

Any discussion of infant baptism needs to begin with the right question: "Are children of Christian parents members of the covenant community, and should they therefore receive the sign of entrance into that community?" When the question is asked in this way, the burden of proof falls upon the "believers only" side of the discussion. And yet evidence for this view is lacking. If, however, we press for evidence from the covenantal baptism perspective, we discover a fourfold stream of testimony. God chooses to work according to his covenant, and we find that this covenant of grace is a thread that unifies all of Scripture. In the Old Testament era, children received the sign and seal of initiation into the covenant people of God through circumcision. God has not changed. The plan of salvation hasn't changed. The promises haven't changed. Thus, unless God tells us otherwise, we expect children to receive the sign and seal of baptism as they are initiated into God's covenant people during the New Testament era. And the theological testimony of the Scriptures reinforces the truths conveyed by covenantal baptism. The testimony of the early church and of the church throughout the centuries shows that covenantal baptism has been practiced historically and universally. Though Scripture provides no proof text for either "believers only" or covenantal baptism, wherever we look, we find more evidence for the latter.

Questions for Further Reflection

1. What crucial question must we ask regarding children's baptism? What makes it the crucial question?
2. If the baptistic position is to be believed, what fundamental change of status have covenant children undergone?
3. Why would it matter if this change of status happened?

4. Why do you think no one verse or single account in the Scriptures sufficiently answers the question of who should receive baptism?
5. Identify the fourfold stream of testimony that this chapter presented. Are any of these streams of testimony new or encouraging to you?

3

BLESSINGS TO THE CHILDREN

When my father's side of the family would gather for a reunion, he and his brothers and sisters would travel to my grandparents' home. These aunts and uncles would also bring their children—my cousins—in tow. These were rare events, and so we relished the time to play with one another. However, I remember watching my dad and his siblings play board and card games together. I would hear them laughing loudly, and it always felt like I was missing out on the "real fun." I would hover at the edge of the room, anxious to join my dad, aunts, and uncles at the table. But they would say time and again, "Jason, this is for adults. Go play with the other kids." I belonged, and they weren't rudely dismissive; but I didn't *quite* belong. I could watch and even laugh, from a distance, but not *quite* join in.

While that isn't a perfect analogy, I'm concerned that too often the experience of covenant children in our churches echoes this scene. We bring them close but not *quite* close enough. We teach them to pray, bring them to worship services, encourage them to sing, and require them to attend Sunday school, but we communicate that they don't *quite* belong. The blessings of Christ are not *quite* for them—or at least not yet.

However, in the Scriptures we witness something different. Christ welcomes children, and even includes them in the blessings he offers, as we saw briefly in chapter 2. Let us return to that famous scene from Luke 18 and consider it a little more closely. While it is a scene often pictured in artwork, it is more often than not pictured wrongly. In paintings, Jesus sits on a rock and a flock of elementary school–aged children gather around him. That is not the scene that we find in Luke 18, though. Instead, Jesus is being mobbed by a group of parents who Luke tells us have "infants" in their arms. The same word is used in Luke 2:12 to describe the baby Jesus who is wrapped in swaddling clothes and lying in a manger. Peter employs the same term, as well, when he tells his readers in 1 Peter 2:2 that they should, "like newborn infants, long for the pure spiritual milk." These children being presented to Jesus are small. Very small. Infants.

The verb for "were bringing" in Luke 18 conveys the sense of a continual bringing. This was ongoing—a constant barrage of infants being thrust before Jesus so that he might "touch them," as Luke says in verse 15.

And Luke says that these parents were continually bringing "even infants" to Jesus. Why emphasize that they were "even" infants? The Greco-Roman world of the New Testament thought very little of children—and especially infants. Maybe this was due to the high mortality rate that children suffered and therefore a way for adults to safeguard their hearts from getting too attached to them. Maybe it stemmed from pure adult self-centeredness. Regardless of the reason, however, children were simply viewed as those who were "not adults." They didn't possess the value that they eventually would as grown-ups. In fact, they didn't possess value at all until they could at least help with their family farm or business. Due to this low regard for children, infanticide and child abandonment were rampant in the Roman world.

The disciples were citizens of their age—here, they see a throng of parents bringing infants to Jesus and strongly rebuke them. Why should mere infants drain Jesus's time and energy? These "not adults" are serving as a distraction from things that matter more. He can't be bothered to bless these insignificant children.

Yet Jesus rebukes the disciples in return. Why? Because our Lord is never too important, too busy, too taxed, or too powerful for the least among us. "But Jesus called them to him, saying, 'Let the children come to me, and do not hinder them, for to such belongs the kingdom of God'" (Luke 18:16).

Now, make no mistake—the disciples, though they were people of their time, should have known that Jesus would welcome these children. This was not a new approach God was taking, and it shouldn't be a novel approach for his people. Because God has always welcomed children. As we saw in the previous chapter, children have always been part of the covenant community. God invites them into his presence, and they receive his blessings. Christ is not doing something new here.[1] And, just as this has always been true of God and was true of Christ's earthly ministry, so a healthy church refuses to neglect or to simply entertain or babysit its children; rather, it continually brings them to Christ and follows his command not to "hinder them." It seeks to see them blessed by him.

Our children are set apart and distinct. They differ from the children of the world. We surround them with prayer, engage them in worship, and shine our witness before them. We put them in the way of God's means of grace as they sit under the Word, learn the faith, enjoy the fellowship of God's people, and delight in the blessing of having Christian parents. They are prayed for, witnessed to, and called forth. They know a true privilege in this world that many children do not enjoy. In a word, they are blessed. And baptism signifies this blessing even as it conveys blessing.

In a real sense, baptism is a naming ceremony.[2] It is administered in the name of the triune Godhead: Father, Son, and Holy Spirit. As Scottish Reformed theologian, pastor, and scholar Sinclair Ferguson stated, "Our great High Priest, Jesus Christ, pronounces the blessing. We are baptized into his name, with a view to his saving resources, his possession, authority and fellowship."[3] As Jesus welcomed children during his earthly ministry and blessed them, so the church continues to welcome children in the name of Jesus and see them blessed. They are baptized into the name of the triune God and receive all the benefits of Christ as they receive him in faith.

What Does Baptizing Our Children Not Mean?

Does the fact that our covenant children are set apart, distinct, and different from the children of the world mean that they are saved? Not necessarily. We believe that God normatively works to save our covenant children, and so we have great hope—but baptism does not generate faith. Just as circumcision did not cause salvation, baptism does not cause salvation. To our great sadness, some who receive this sign reject the covenant that it signifies. Ishmaels and Esaus exist among the Isaacs and Jacobs.

As pastor and theologian Ligon Duncan said, "Nowhere in the Bible will you find a covenant sign [sacrament] which *effects* a relationship. A covenant sign always *reflects* a relationship."[4] The sacrament signifies blessing to those who, by grace, believe. But to those who do not believe, it will serve as a witness against them, because, despite all the benefits they enjoyed as members of the covenant community, they rejected the God of that covenant.

All the blessings that the sacrament signifies for eight-day-old children may be realized when they are eight years old or eighty-eight years old. As Calvin wonderfully said, "The sacraments properly fulfill their office only when the Spirit, that inward teacher, comes to them, by whose power alone hearts are penetrated and affections moved and our souls opened for the sacraments to enter in. If the Spirit [is] lacking, the sacraments can accomplish nothing more in our minds than the splendor of the sun shining upon blind eyes, or a voice sounding in deaf ears."[5] Those who receive the sign need the Spirit to work in them and teach them inwardly in order for all that it signifies to be sealed to them.

Grace is granted through the sacraments. When we think of grace, we tend to think of it as a substance or thing in and of itself. But grace is not a thing. Rather, it is the person of Christ Jesus and all the benefits that are attached to him, which the Spirit applies. The Westminster Shorter Catechism states that "a sacrament is a holy ordinance instituted by Christ, wherein, by sensible signs, *Christ*, and the benefits of the new covenant, are represented, sealed, and applied to believers."[6] Thus, the sacrament of baptism does not confer some "substance" of grace to the baptized child. Rather, it—like the Word—communicates Christ and all his benefits to an elect child.

In this way, Reformed theology stands in stark

contrast to the Roman Catholic view of baptism, which asserts that the simple act confers grace itself (*ex opera operato*[7]). We believe that Christ is communicated not by the act but by the Spirit who works through the act. The waters of baptism provide nothing but a public sprinkling with water if the Spirit is not at work. As J. V. Fesko summarizes, "Stated succinctly, the Roman Catholic Church believes that grace is a thing doled out by priests, whereas the Reformed church believes grace is *a person* to whom a believer is sovereignly united by the Spirit. Only God through Christ and the Spirit orchestrates such a holy union. Man is incapable of such a miraculous feat."[8]

The Word does not confer salvation to everyone within audible range when it is preached. No Christian believes this, or evangelism would consist simply of sneaking into neighborhoods at night, rolling in a few loudspeakers, and blaring John 3:16. The Spirit must attend the Word to make it effectual unto salvation by grace through faith. Baptism, which has been described by the Reformers as the visible Word, is made effectual in the same way. Calvin said that a person needs faith in order to receive the blessings of the sacraments. He compared the sacraments to wine being poured out. If wine is poured onto a closed container, the wine flows away and disappears. The container must be opened, or the wine will splash upon the outside while the inside remains empty.[9] The Spirit makes the waters of baptism effectual by grace alone through our faith alone.

What Are the Blessings of Baptism, Then?

Blessings of the Call to Faith

It helps to remind ourselves that believer's baptism and covenantal baptism are not wholly different. There weren't two kinds of circumcision, nor are there two kinds of baptism. There is only one baptism (see Eph. 4:5), and it always "signifies union with Christ, purifying from the pollution of sin by regeneration of the Spirit, and purifying from the guilt of sin by the blood of Christ."[10] As Murray goes on to state, "As a sign and seal of such grace the sign and seal must have the same efficacy for infants as for adults."[11]

So what does it benefit infants to be given this sign when they are so young? Like circumcision before it, baptism calls out to those who receive it. It forever marks them as having belonged to the covenant community, reminding them that they have heard the covenant promises and pleading with them all the days of their lives to believe, to have faith in Christ, to look to this God of promise. Baptism is "always there bearing witness to the will of the Father, the work of the Son, and the ministry of the Spirit."[12] In this sense, infant baptism serves alongside the Word to proclaim to the child who receives it their need for the Spirit to work the twin graces of repentance and faith within them. Through baptism, the child enters the visible church—by being identified on earth as part of the covenant community—but only through faith and repentance does that child become a member of the *invisible* church, thereby joining the ranks of true believers and having the blessings of the covenant that were signified in their baptism now sealed to them by God. Therefore, baptism seals those to whom God grants the gift of faith.

In this way, Reformed theology clearly distinguishes itself from other traditions by maintaining that the sacraments are a means of grace (contra most baptistic, Anabaptist, and "Zwinglian" traditions) and yet that "their efficacy resides not in the sacramental elements or in the sacramental action, nor in the character or intention of the one who administers them [contra the Roman Catholic Church], but in Christ's blessing and the work of the Spirit in their beneficiaries. They are means of grace only to those who fulfill the conditions of the covenant of which they are signs and seals"[13]—the "conditions" here referring to repentance and faith. Therefore, from the moment our children receive the sacrament of baptism, we should point them to what that sacrament signified for them. We should plead and pray for them to believe and trust in the God whose name they were baptized into.

Maybe the sweetest moment I have ever witnessed in ministry occurred in our elders' meeting room at the church. An individual whom, years earlier, the church had excommunicated—had formally disciplined by excluding her from the church and its benefits—was now coming back to the elders to confess her sin and ask for forgiveness. When asked what had led her to do so after all those years, she reminded us of a pastoral letter she had received. The letter had reminded her of what she had heard preached for years, of the danger her soul was in, and of her need for repentance and faith. It had clearly articulated the fact that Christ's grace is always sufficient to cover all our sins. Even though the elders had sent her the letter when she had been excommunicated for her unrepentant sin, most of the men had forgotten it—but she had not. As the years had passed, the letter had not let her rest. After she had received it, kept it, and placed it in the top drawer of her dresser, there it had sat—and kept calling out to her, if you will, to turn in repentance and faith. She knew it was there and couldn't ignore it.

Baptism sits upon the individual the way that letter had sat in her dresser drawer. And as it sits there, it continually calls out, "Remember all that you heard. Christ's grace is more than sufficient. Believe and repent."

Blessings of the Call to Faithfulness

Baptism calls our children not only to faith but to faithfulness. Members of the covenant have covenantal obligations as well as blessings—obligations to be faithful and obedient to Christ.[14] Therefore, the sacraments not only demonstrate that the Lord promises to cancel our debt to him and reconcile us to himself but also that the individual who is marked by the sacrament is binding himself or herself to seek piety and holiness for God's glory.

Question 167 of the Westminster Larger Catechism

asks, "How is our baptism to be improved by us?" The word *improved* may seem like an odd word choice in our day, but the authors of the catechism, the Westminster divines, meant that we are to apply throughout our lives what our baptism signifies by living in accordance with what that baptism entails. They first point out that improving our baptism is a duty that many people neglect and yet a necessary one that should mark our entire Christian lives. And this duty should come to our minds in particular when we face temptation or witness the baptism of others.

The divines provide quite a long list of things for us to consider as we seek to "improve" our baptism. We should remember the privileges and benefits that baptism confers and seals as well as the solemn vow made in our baptism. We should be humble as we consider our sinfulness and the way we are walking contrary to the grace of baptism, and we should commit to grow in grace instead.

The catechism helpfully encourages us to "[grow] up to assurance of pardon of sin, and of all other blessings sealed to us in that sacrament; by drawing strength from the death and resurrection of Christ, into whom we are baptized, for the mortifying of sin, and quickening of grace; and by endeavoring to live by faith, to have our conversation in holiness and righteousness, as those that have therein given up their names to Christ; and to walk in brotherly love, as being baptized by the same Spirit into one body." Notice that we draw strength from the death and resurrection of Christ, into whom we were baptized, to enable our efforts to live for him. Baptism reminds, encourages, and exhorts us to live in faithfulness.

Have I improved upon my baptism? I would ask you to consider that question yourself, using this catechism answer as a helpful tool to think and pray through. Have the past twenty years, thirty years, forty years, fifty years of sitting under the preached Word, knowing Christ as my Savior, dwelling in the church, and hearing the promises of God increasingly affected my life? Am I growing? What have I to show in the areas of character development, holiness, and maturity in Christ as I've been looking to him more? Have I grown in my knowledge of him? Have I grown in my affection for him? In my love for others?

Striving and resting are twin virtues within the Christian life. The sacrament of baptism calls us to that truth. The Christian life is all of grace, and yet we are to improve upon our baptism as well.

Blessings of Church Discipline

Baptized children are under the care of the elders of the church. They are members of the church— non-communing members who are not yet admitted to the Lord's Table, but members nonetheless. Therefore, they enjoy all the benefits of that membership, and those include church discipline.

The Reformers often spoke of the three marks of the church: the preaching of the Word, the right administration of the sacraments, and the exercise of church discipline. The Word governs the waters of baptism and the Table, the sacraments reinforce the truth of the Word, and church discipline safeguards the recipients and the means themselves by ensuring, as much as possible, that the means are not used in an unworthy manner. The relationship between baptism and church discipline is one of the great benefits the covenant child receives. As Fesko helpfully states, "When the church administers baptism, it must continually keep the theology of the cross and the recipient's sacramental relation to Christ in His death at the fore. This means that for all baptismal recipients, the church must be willing, in love, to exercise church discipline, even upon children who are baptized and live in a way contrary to the way of the cross of Christ."[15]

The idea of church discipline scares many Christians today. And in many cases this fear is understandable—many people have witnessed church leadership mishandle discipline and damage the church as a result. Others fear an overly authoritative group of elders who would constantly look over congregants' shoulders. But church discipline, when rightly administered, is a source of blessing, not fear.

On Sunday mornings, I often look out over the congregation I serve and remind myself of the responsibility I have, as an elder, not just for my own children but for all the children of our church. My fellow elders and I pray through the congregation, which includes praying for its children, because they are members of our church whom we bear responsibility for. We pursue these children when they go astray and grieve as we lovingly discipline any who turn their back upon the Lord of their baptisms. And when they repent, we welcome them home as prodigal children. Watchful care for the souls of our children is essential in the life of the church. They receive this blessing, which is tied to their baptism as members of the church.

Blessings of Assurance

When our children place their faith in Christ, baptism serves as a continual means of grace that grants them the assurance of God's eternal promises. Like a seal pressed into wax on parchment, baptism seals these promises to our children, even as it does to us. It impresses upon the soul truths such as "You are God's. You are forgiven. You are cut off from the first Adam. You are united to the second Adam. The old you died, and the new you has been resurrected with Christ. You are his, and he is yours."

Our adversary, Satan, knows that if he can take away our assurance, we will lose our courage in the fight of faith. Martin Luther, the prominent Reformer, knew a great deal about this tactic. When the devil tempted him to despair of his salvation, Luther would remind his adversary (and himself) of his baptism and what it signified and sealed. He is recorded as saying, "The only way to drive away the Devil is through faith in Christ, by saying: 'I have been baptized, I am a Christian.'"[16] He rightly placed his faith in this One whom he found himself united to, washed by, and forever secured in. Every time we witness baptism being administered, the hearts of the faith-filled should well up and their eyes should fill with tears at the secure promises that are theirs in Christ Jesus.

Conclusion

Is it necessary for our covenant children to receive baptism in order to be saved? No. But the blessings that they enjoy when they are baptized, and which baptism signifies for them, should encourage us to bring them to the baptismal font. Ultimately we want them to know, see, and delight in Christ, who values them, blesses them, and says, "Let the children come to me." Baptism serves as one of these blessings he has granted our children as a confirmation of his love for and blessings to them. May we put them in the way of his grace and continually point them to his blessings—blessings that are great, because our Christ is great.

Questions for Further Reflection

1. What does baptizing our covenant children not mean?
2. How will baptism serve as a witness against those who have received the sacrament but do not believe?

3. Is covenantal baptism a holdover from Roman Catholicism? How does Reformed theology differ from a Catholic understanding of the sacrament?

4. If baptism isn't necessary for the salvation of our children, then why baptize them? What are the blessings they receive from it?

5. How does baptism encourage a person to be faithful over the course of his or her life?

BLESSINGS TO THE PARENTS

I love that when children are baptized in a Presbyterian church, their parents take vows. They hear the covenant promises of God and then reply to them with vows that are rooted in faith. Covenant promises are accompanied by covenantal responsibilities.

The Presbyterian Church in America's book of church order contains three vows for parents to answer in the affirmative.[1] These or similar vows are employed in most Presbyterian or Reformed churches. In this chapter I will explore each of these three vows and the blessings that are communicated through them—as well as one final blessing for parents whose children have wandered from the faith.

The Blessing of Remembering Our Children's Need

The first vow is "Do you acknowledge your child's need of the cleansing blood of Jesus Christ, and the renewing grace of the Holy Spirit?" This question asks the

Christian parents who are taking the vow to affirm that even though their child is cute and they love their child dearly as he or she is, that child has the greatest of all needs. It sets all parenting in perspective. Our children's greatest need is for the cleansing blood of Jesus Christ and the renewing grace of the Holy Spirit. Being ignorant of this dire need causes us to be casual or flippant about our children's salvation—or even to disregard it. Those who hold a baptistic view rightfully point out that there are no grandchildren in the family of God. Indeed! We long for our children to be God's children. Every parent of every covenant child stands before the watching eyes of the congregation as well as God to affirm that the cute, cuddly blessing of a child they hold in their arms has been born into this world a wretched sinner. The child, like every one of us, possesses the greatest of needs. A knowledge of this will inform and direct parenting like nothing else. Christian parents know that, though we may provide them with shelter, clothing, food, and even a loving and affirming home, if we are not putting our children in the way of gospel grace, their greatest need remains unaddressed.

The Blessing of Faith and Rest

This is where the second question must quickly follow the first. It asks, "Do you claim God's covenant promises in [your child's] behalf, and do you look in faith to the

Lord Jesus Christ for [your child's] salvation as you do for your own?"

God is a covenant-keeping God. Though there are no grandchildren in the body of Christ, he is a God both to us and to our children; we can look in faith to him. This child is not without hope, and neither are his or her parents. The child's greatest need lies beyond our greatest abilities. But our God is our child's God. What rest is found in this knowledge! Truly, baptism serves as a means of grace not only to our covenant children but to us, their parents.

We parents of covenant children can find rest as we look to the waters of baptism. God is not just for us but also for our children. "This promise is for you and for your children," God tells Abraham, and Peter reiterates this truth at Pentecost. It is God's promise, and it is his work. Yet we often forget this. Our Christian faith becomes quickly confused. We argue incessantly, and rightly, that our own personal salvation is wholly a work of God but then act as though the salvation of our children is the result of our work.[2] Let us remind ourselves that both our own salvation and our children's salvation lie in the hands of God. They need grace—saving grace. And saving grace comes only from God—a truth that the sacrament of baptism represents and signifies.

This vow requires a true surrendering of our children to God. This is the chief similarity between covenantal baptisms and baby dedications, which otherwise are two vastly different things. Baby dedications are sweet moments in a service for recognizing the parents' intention to raise their child to know Christ, whereas covenantal baptism is a means of grace to a child (as we saw in the previous chapter) and the child's parents. It is more than a dedication—and yet, as we bring our children to the waters of baptism, we do dedicate them. Doing this is a public acknowledgment that we, as Christian parents, consider our children differently from how parents of the world consider their children. The most precious of blessings in our lives, we devote to God. We are stewards of these little lives he has given us, and we acknowledge that they are his more than they are ours. We entrust them to him—and rest accompanies this trust.

I remember when this was first pressed home to me. My wife and I had desired children for quite some time, but for whatever reason the Lord never blessed us with biological children. After years of battling infertility, we began the adoption process. We had always wanted to adopt, as well, but we thought this would happen after we had already borne a few biological children—the Lord, however, had other plans. We went through the long process of adopting a child (and, later, a second) from Taiwan. The next couple of years involved a lot of paperwork, a lot of visits to governmental offices, various strangers coming and inspecting our home, and a fair amount of expense. Finally, one day, we received a phone call. The person on the other end of the line informed us that a little baby girl by the name of Hsi-en had been chosen for adoption into our family. We were elated. In fact, that is an understatement for the ages. For the next few anxious months, we planned, prayed, hoped, and longed for that next phone call that would tell us we could travel to finally meet our daughter and bring her home. Finally it came. We booked plane tickets, packed our bags, and headed out the door. After twenty hours in the air, a quick taxi ride to the hotel, and a quicker shower, off we went to the orphanage.

There we met our sweet, chubby-cheeked little girl, whom we had known only through pictures. This was our daughter! We were parents at last. We spent a week finishing the government paperwork and procedures, visiting a few sites, and eating some Chinese dumplings. More than anything else, though, we spent time holding, cuddling, making fishy faces at, and delighting in this new eight-month-old baby girl.

After we returned home, life was good—for a few weeks—until it wasn't. My wife called me at the church one day and said that I needed to rush to the hospital. Our daughter had been dealing with a high temperature for a couple of days. We hadn't wanted to overreact as new parents, so we had called the doctor and followed his instructions by giving her mild baths to lower her temperature. But then she had a seizure—and then another. A doctor immediately sent my wife and daughter to the hospital. While she was there, our daughter's temperature spiked to 105.7 degrees. A team of doctors paraded in and out of the room for the next few hours. At one point, there were four different specialists occupying our hospital room and discussing the situation with one another in hushed tones. After running many tests, they hypothesized that she had contracted a disease in Taiwan that they were unfamiliar with.

One doctor took me aside to tell me, in a roundabout way, to brace my wife and myself for the worst. I believe they thought she was going to die—and we feared the same. Then, after many tests, they decided that she might have spinal meningitis. A spinal tap was needed in order to confirm the diagnosis. One of the nurses took me aside and said, "You and your wife can stay in the room, but I would recommend that you wait in the hall while we do this spinal tap. This will be very painful for your daughter, and it will not be easy to watch." So I put my arms around my dear bride and led her to the hallway outside the hospital room. The hallway of a hospital never felt more cold and clinical than at that moment.

I took my wife's hand and began to pray. I hadn't thought through what I was going to say; the words just came tumbling out. In a broken voice, with my wife weeping beside me and my daughter screaming in pain in the background, I heard myself praying, "Our Father, we love this little girl. You know how much we have desired to be parents and how much we adore our daughter. Save her. Keep her life. But, oh Lord, know this: if you choose to take her, we will still believe and trust in you."

I am not a man of unfaltering faith. That prayer existed on my lips only because of God's great love and mercy. It flowed from his grace. In such moments, we all know our limitations—and, equally, his total ability. But, even more, we know his kindness. (In our particular situation, we received kindness upon kindness—it turned out that our daughter had a kidney infection, and she made a full recovery in the days and weeks that followed.) As Christian parents, we can find and experience great rest in the knowledge that our children are in his hands.

If you are like me, you feel much stronger than you truly are. As our Lord said to Peter after his failure in the garden of Gethsemane, "The spirit indeed is willing, but the flesh is weak" (Matt. 26:41). It often takes dark moments, such as the one I experienced in the hospital or as Peter experienced in the garden, to remind us of our weakness, inability, and utter dependence upon God. And nothing reminds us of this dependence more than the spiritual concerns we have for our children. If I cannot heal my daughter's body, I know that I certainly cannot heal her soul. Though we may desire to with our entire being, none of us can grant our children new life. This inability calls us to look up to God in our parenting and depend on him. In fact, the walk of faith is one of moving from moment of dependence to moment of dependence. And, though on the surface this appears to be a burden, such dependence actually offers us rest.

The Blessing of Labor

This rest that we can find, however, does not negate our need to strive, as well—hence the third question: "Do you now unreservedly dedicate your child to God, and promise, in humble reliance upon divine grace, that you will endeavor to set before [your child] a godly example, that you will pray with and for [your child], that you will teach [your child] the doctrines of our holy religion, and that you will strive, by all the means of God's appointment, to bring [your child] up in the nurture and admonition of the Lord?"

As we rely "upon divine grace," we also "endeavor" and "strive" with and for our children's souls. The family serves as the most fertile soil in which the seeds of gospel truth can bear fruit. And, as this soil is softened by the rains of God's grace and warmed by the rays of his mercy, Christian parents tend to it as well through the nurture they provide.

That's why it's important for us to seek to raise our children in "the nurture and admonition of the Lord," as we promise to do by taking this vow. All our parenting is done in the hope that they will know, trust, and delight in the Lord whom we love. We commit to not allow our children to mature without hearing God's covenant promises and being called to seize upon them. Evangelism is a way of life for Christian parents. We continually direct our children to the goodness of God and the covenant promises he has made to us in Christ Jesus and always call our children not to bank upon the fact that their parents are Christians but to realize that they must place their own personal faith in the Lord Jesus Christ.

Presbyterian pastor Dane Ortlund said this well when he wrote, "At the center, our job [as parents] is to show our kids that even our best love is a shadow of a greater love. To put a shaper edge on it: to make the tender heart of Christ irresistible and unforgettable."[3]

I love to hear a new member who joins our church say, "I was raised in a Christian home; I don't remember a day in which I did not know Christ." This is the testimony of children who were blessed with parents who loved Christ, modeled him before them, talked often of him, prayed with and for them, and brought them to church week in and week out. People who say this often point back to having been baptized in the church and thus raised in the church.

The best testimonies of Christian faith are the most boring ones. Often it is the drug-addicted, philandering sluggard who is converted to Christ who receives the most attention—and that is a wonderful miracle! Let us celebrate such a conversion with thanksgiving and joy. Yet a boring testimony is even more miraculous! It is the story of one who was born into this world a sinner—a child of Adam—but who nonetheless cannot recall a day that he or she did not know the Lord. What a mercy!

To possess such a testimony is impossible, however, without being raised in a faithful and faith-filled Christian home by parents (or a parent) who strive, by the power of the Spirit, to live for and to the glory of Christ. Such a home cannot guarantee this kind of testimony; but what *is* guaranteed is that no such testimony has ever flowed from a home that did not have at least one striving Christian parent.

Samuel Miller, the great Old Princeton professor and preacher, once commented,

> The truth is, if infant baptism were properly improved; if the profession which it includes, and the obligations which it imposes, were suitably appreciated and followed up, it would have few opponents. I can no more doubt, if this were done, that it would be blessed to the saving conversion of thousands of our young people, than I can doubt the faithfulness of a covenant God. Yes, infant baptism is of God, but the fault lies in the conduct of its advocates. The inconsistency of its friends, has done more to discredit it, than all the arguments of its opposers, a hundred fold.[4]

Though the salvation of our children is God's work, he does not encourage us to be slothful. Even as we look to him, we are also to strive for him. The soil is not ours to lay, but it is ours to tend. We cannot cause the seed to take root, but we are to sow that seed. We cannot shower the ground with rain, but we are to prepare for the rain. And when the fruit comes forth, while it will not be our doing, we are still to harvest it. Let us treat, train, and tutor our children as members of the covenant community.

We all need encouragement in this regard. Below are some suggestions for how we can labor and strive well for the sake of our covenant children.

Remind Your Covenant Children of Their Baptism

The Lord has given you the gift of baptism to be a wonderful means of grace in your children's lives. Just as Abraham could tell his children, "You have the mark of being born into the covenant people of God," so we can tell our children, "You were baptized as a sign that you are numbered among the covenant people of God." We have in our hands one of the greatest means for evangelism. "You were baptized. Do you know what that means?" Every time your children witness a baptism in a worship service, a ready-made field for their questions opens: "Daddy, Mommy, was I baptized?" And it's a ready-made field for you to sow seeds in response: "Yes—do you know what baptism means? Have you placed your faith in Jesus? Are you washed by his blood?"

Pray with and for Your Covenant Children

As we raise our covenant children, we employ the means that God gives us for promoting and encouraging their spiritual growth. One of those means is prayer. If we knew what we accomplish for the sake of the kingdom when we are on our knees, we would be tempted never to rise. "The . . . prayer of a righteous man availeth much" (James 5:16 KJV)—and so the prayer of a righteous parent availeth much. Pray for God to grant your children faith; plead for them to grow in godliness; intercede for their tender souls. Lift them up before the throne of grace and entrust your children to God. Parents who pray for their children bless their children; a minute spent in prayer for your covenant children is never a minute wasted. And even as you pray for them, pray with your children. Teach them the joys of communing with God in prayer. Some of the most intimate moments a family can enjoy is when they are united in spirit on bended knee. There is power in your children hearing your own intimate conversations with the Lord and seeing your love for him. And remember the promises that your children's baptisms signified, dear Christian parent, as you pray with and for them. These promises should saturate your prayers for them— and it will further serve to benefit them if they hear these promises being prayed.

Practice Family Worship in Your Home[5]

Your Christian home is to be a little church—one that is centered upon Christ and therefore the worship of Christ. The regular routine of gathering around the Word, praying together, and daring to sing with one another shines as one of the greatest blessings of being brought up as a covenant child in a covenant home. I pray that all our children would look back upon their years of youth and be able to say that they lived a life of worship in their homes.

Call Your Covenant Children to Repentance and Faith

Christian parents must keep putting their children in the way of God's means of grace and keep trusting that he will work in their lives. He entrusts these children to our Christian nurture even as we entrust them to his saving work. Continually set the grace of God before your children's minds and hearts as you remind them of their need for faith. Teach them to set their hearts upon things that are above and not on earth. Impress over and over upon their souls that God's grace is sufficient to cover all their sins. And tell them, time and again, that their baptism is a sign of that truth.

Catechize Your Children

Instill in your children the deep theological truths of our faith. The historic spiritual discipline of catechizing serves as one of the most proven, helpful, and easy ways to accomplish this goal in the lives of our children. Most people would be surprised by how easily small children can memorize truths this way that will stick with them and inform their lives for decades to come.

Years ago, when my daughter (whom I spoke of earlier in this chapter) was ten years old or so, our front doorbell rang. I walked to the front door and found two Jehovah's Witnesses on my front porch. I was their evangelism target for the morning—but little did they know that they had suddenly become mine! They began by asking me a couple of questions; and, as I have done numerous times, I told these two kind women that I was more than happy to answer any and all questions that they wanted to ask—but that after they asked me ten questions, I would like the privilege of asking them four questions that they had to be willing to answer in turn. They happily agreed.

After fifteen minutes of answering their questions, I asked mine: "Do you believe that Jesus is the Son of God?" "Oh yes," quickly came their answer. "Do you believe that Jesus is God?" And again they quickly replied: "We believe he is *a* god." (That article is all-important for Jehovah's Witnesses.) I then asked, "Do you think you believe in the same Jesus—the same Son of God—I believe in?" They replied, "Yes, of course." Then the clincher: "Do you believe the Son of God has always existed?" This answer came a little less quickly. The older of the women replied, "No; he was the first of God's creation."

Now, my daughter was sitting in the room playing with some toys, though I was unaware of her presence. But that very quickly changed. Upon hearing that last reply, with all her ten-year-old vigor she jumped up, ran to my side, and said to the older woman, "That is not true. God is a spirit, infinite, eternal, and unchangeable in his being, wisdom, power, holiness, justice, goodness, and truth." Out of the mouths of babes.

What had happened? She knew untruth when she heard it. How did she know it? Because she had sown the theology of the Scriptures regarding the very person of God in her young ten-year-old mind by memorizing a portion of the Westminster Shorter Catechism. Time spent catechizing our children is time spent well.

Bring Them Week In and Week Out to Corporate Worship

While it is not always easy to do so, bringing our children to corporate worship is central to Christian parenting. Why? Because corporate worship is the most important part of the life that the covenant community shares together—and children are part of this covenant community. God chooses to meet with his people, through his Word and his Spirit, in the context of corporate worship. It is in that context that we hear the Word read and preached, join our voices in song, offer united prayer, confess our corporate sin, partake of the Lord's Table, and administer baptism. During corporate worship, God ministers to us through these ordinary means of grace (the Word, the sacraments, and prayer)—and, when our children attend corporate worship alongside us, they dwell in the midst of these effectual means of grace. The more we place them in the way of the means of grace, the better opportunity their souls have to encounter the God of grace.[6]

Talk Often of Christ and the Things of Christ

Talk often of Christ. Seize moments throughout the day to talk about your faith. Don't reserve Christ and the things of God for when you're driving to church. Christ is your friend, and your children need to see that he is constantly upon your mind. Help them to consider him as someone who is ever present—to stop and pray to him during the routines of life, thank him for his blessings, and confess sin. Ask them questions throughout the week that will get them to consider Christ and his Word. As the law commanded parents to do with the statutes of God, "Teach them diligently to your children, and . . . talk of them when you sit in your house, and when you walk by the way, and when you lie down, and when you rise" (Deut. 6:7). You can sow the truth of Christ in your children's lives using the simplest of conversations. And who knows what simple moment here or there might be the very moment our Lord uses to seal truth upon their souls. So talk of Christ.

The Blessing of Hope

I realize that many people have raised their children to know Christ and yet have not seen the fruit of doing so. Grief fills the hearts of some Christian parents—their children are not walking on the path of righteousness, and they watch as their children wander and, in some cases, outright reject Christ. I know parents who this has happened to—and I grieve for them. They brought up their children in the faith: their children attended Sunday school, participated in corporate worship and Vacation Bible School, went to youth group. These parents did not shy away from sharing the faith at home, and they attempted to surround their children with good and godly friends. They sought to model Christ before them. Yet now their children are living lives of unbelief.

If this is true of you, then first let me say, "I'm sorry." This is some of the hardest ground that we traverse in this life. May God grant you comfort and solace under the shadow of his wings. I'm praying that even now for you, as I write these words: "Lord, help any parents who are weighed down with grief or guilt, as they read these words, to know your comfort and grace." Your God keeps count of your tossings upon your bed at night and puts every one of your tears in his bottle (see Ps. 56:8). Your sorrow is not lost on him.

And that is not all. There is comfort in God's promises for you, as well. Though your sorrow is great, your God is greater still. Keep reminding yourself of the years you have spent sowing the truth of God's Word in your children's lives. You prayed for them, brought them to church week in and week out, and pointed them to Christ through your conversations and actions. You brought them to him. Did you do it perfectly? No. What parent has? But you sowed the seeds of truth. And that effort was not wasted—God promises that his Word will not return void (see Isa. 55:11) and that it is living and active (see Heb. 4:12). The truth that your children heard will call out to them for the rest of their lives. The truth that marked them in their baptism will echo through the corridors of their lives. So keep praying. Like the persistent widow, keep praying until your petition is realized. As the stalwart Reformed theologian Charles Hodge stated, there is "an intimate and divinely established connexion between the faith of parents and the salvation of their children; such a connexion as authorizes them to plead God's promises, and to expect with confidence, that through his blessing on their faithful efforts, their children will grow up the children of God."[7] Do not shy away from enlisting others in the church to pray for your children, either.

Above all, continue to hope. Not one of our covenant children is too far gone for God's grace to be able to reach him or her. Never allow our adversary to sow a lie in your mind to the contrary. No matter how great her sin, no matter how hard his heart, no matter how firm her resolve, no matter how strident his tongue, no matter how advanced her years, our Lord can work the miracle of conversion for a covenant child in the blink of an eye. So keep praying with hope. He is a covenant-keeping God. "O Father, this was one of the children of the covenant community. Lord, this child is marked by baptism. Save this child, I pray! Make my child your child. I know that you love me and hear my prayers, so I will keep praying and hoping and trusting."

Conclusion

Covenantal baptism serves as a wonderful blessing for Christian parents. The Lord has given us good gifts through not only our children but also this sacrament that is to mark them. It provides not only hope but confidence. It encourages us to be faithful in our parenting even as it demands that we rest. Our God has declared that his promises are not only for us but for our children; let's live, pray, and believe this. He is worthy of our trust.

Questions for Further Reflection

1. Why do parents take vows when their children are baptized?
2. Identify and explain the benefits that parents receive when their children are baptized.
3. How can Christian parents maintain a balance between rest and labor as they long to see faith in their children? What does doing so look like?
4. How can you use your child's baptism as a practical way to remind him or her to look to Christ in faith?
5. What is one thing you could begin doing in your home in order to foster more regular discussion and contemplation of Christ and all the blessings we have in him?

BLESSINGS TO THE CONGREGATION

The sacraments belong to the covenant community. Therefore, we rightly and normatively administer them in the midst of the assembled church body. Each person in the congregation is blessed by being able to observe the sacraments taking place in the midst of God's people in the local church. In fact, I would contend that when a congregation witnesses the baptism of one of its own, it is showered with blessings as it participates in one of the sweetest and most impactful moments a Christian community can share.

The Blessing of the Picture Given

To witness any baptism is a blessing—whether the recipient is an adult or child, the covenant blessings that the baptism signifies encourage the soul. When an adult comes by profession of faith to the waters of baptism, grace is on display; our hearts should leap for joy and our faith be fed with encouragement. But something beautiful shines more poignantly in the picture that a small child presents by receiving the covenant sign and seal. Nothing in the world appears more helpless than an infant. Her frame is small and fragile. She has two legs but can't walk. Two arms lie at her side, but she can't reach. She is, in a word, helpless. All she can do is cry out in need. Could anything serve as a more beautiful picture of the need for grace?

The baptism of a covenant child reinforces the priority of grace—not only over works but also over faith. We are each as helpless, in a spiritual sense, as this child is in a physical sense—in fact, even more so. During a baptism, the entire congregation beholds the most precious of pictures that can serve as a reminder that grace precedes all. Grace precedes effort. Grace precedes desire. Grace even precedes faith. We cannot make our way to God any more than the child who is being baptized can make his or her way across the room. We cannot conjure up faith or even seek salvation. But the beauty of the gospel is that what we cannot do, God does. What we cannot achieve, God secures. His grace comes to our helpless souls before our souls can come to him. Baptism wonderfully reminds us that faith does not beget grace but, instead, that grace begets faith. And when the waters of baptism flow over a child's head, the congregation is reminded once again that our salvation is all of grace.

The Blessing of the Duty Required

The book of church order of the denomination that I serve contains a question for the pastor to ask the congregation each time a covenant child is baptized—a question that, no doubt, would seem odd to anyone outside the church: "Do you as a congregation undertake the responsibility of assisting the parents in the Christian nurture of this child?"[1] Just as the old African proverb says that "it takes a village to raise a child," this question presses our congregation to affirm what it takes to raise a covenant child: a church. An entire church. Why make this vow every time a child is baptized in our church? Because the child who is baptized isn't just the child of the parents who are presenting him. This child has been born into the world as a covenant child. He or she exists as part of our covenant community—part of our church.

This is no idle vow for a congregation to make. I always ask the members of the congregation that I serve to stand while they make the vow with one voice, because it speaks to our solidarity as a covenant community. Each and every child in our community matters to all of us, and this baptismal vow that we take illustrates this. It illustrates the way in which we, as a community, seek to provide an environment in which each and every covenant child may come to saving faith and grow in that faith. And we seek not only to foster such an environment but also to model before each covenant child what it looks like to live in union with Christ. "When the church is truly one in this effort, a child is surrounded and embraced by the testimony of Christ at every turn in life. Thus, the church becomes God's instrument of presenting the reality of himself to the mind and heart of the child. A child with such an experience, fostered at his baptism and nourished throughout his life by a mature body of believers, breathes the truths of grace as naturally and unconsciously as he breathes air."[2]

Some people who stand in our congregation have matured beyond childrearing years, and yet they still make this vow. Others don't have children of their own but still stand and declare this promise. Regardless of our individual circumstances, we all take this vow as an acknowledgment that the children in the sanctuary, downstairs in the Sunday school classrooms, and out in the hall need each of us. We exist as these children's family. Our godly example before them matters. Our friendship with them influences them. They benefit from our love.

One of my favorite things to observe in the church is when older individuals invest in the smallest members of our congregation. Each church that I have served contains multiple older men and women who embrace this responsibility. What a blessing it is to witness older members of the church sitting and talking with younger covenant children after a Sunday service or in the hallways after a youth event. The children's eyes light up from the attention. They love being loved. I have observed, over the years, that as children mature they often develop a need for an example and voice besides that of their own parents. The older individuals who take the time to provide this are often used by the Lord in momentous ways as these children mature. A moment spent with one of our covenant children is never wasted. Any investment here is an investment for eternity.

Our covenant children need us to be willing to teach them in Sunday school and youth group—and, most importantly, they need the prayers of all the church members. Are you looking for ways to serve in your church? May I recommend a ministry of prayer? You can serve the covenant children of your congregation better on your knees than anywhere else. Few people will know of the contribution you'll be making, but the effects of it could be everlasting. How great an impact would it make on our churches if a dozen people took the church directory and prayed for every child in their congregation, by name, each month? What if twelve mature Christians prayed regularly for all the covenant children? If they prayed for the infants who lack the ability to pray themselves? If they prayed for the toddlers who can't articulate the kinds of prayers that adults can utter? If they prayed for teenagers, who are often distracted from spending time in prayer? And, especially, if they prayed for covenant children who are wandering from the faith? What a blessing our local churches would enjoy. Our children need every one of us, and the vow that we make as a congregation when they are baptized recognizes this truth.

You aren't incredibly gifted? Well, welcome to the club of the "average." Most of us dwell there. Our prayers don't move mountains, charisma doesn't mark our presence, revivals haven't erupted from our evangelism efforts, and crowds aren't flocking to hear us teach. Our faith seems small and our gifts limited. And yet some of the greatest fruit for the sake of the kingdom is borne from the labors of men and women with average talents who labor according to the faith they possess while investing in the smallest members of the covenant community. The Lord often uses the humblest of individuals, who occupy the seemingly smallest of venues, in the most significant of ways. As an encouragement, let me introduce you to someone who influenced me and who reaped eternal dividends by investing in covenant children.

The first church I had the honor of laboring at was a medium-sized church in rural North Carolina. At every church I have attended or served, my practice has been to spend the first six months seeking out the oldest members of the congregation; I find few things to be more important than knowing the history of the church to which I belong. In the conversations I had with individuals of this North Carolina church who were in their seventies and eighties, I kept hearing one particular name: Simon. It seemed that no older man in the congregation was able to tell the history of the church without mentioning Simon. At first I thought he must have served as a pastor early in the life of the church. However, that proved to be far from the case. Everyone said the same things about Simon: he was small in stature, possessed a humble demeanor, seldom spoke in public, and was by all accounts a very "ordinary" layman.

No one would point to Simon as being an incredibly gifted leader, and yet he left a lasting impact on that church that surpassed the legacy of even the most gifted pastors it had enjoyed throughout its history. How did he do this? In a very "average" way. On Sundays, Simon invited the young boys of the church to his house to take afternoon walks. As they would walk through the woods, he would talk to them about trees, plants, birds . . . and Christ. He conversed in an unassuming manner. No weekly agenda, no planning, and no preaching—just an older man spending time with young boys and allowing the Lord to work, in his seemingly simple ways, for profound ends. These men who were now seventy years old all pointed to Simon as being an instrument—if not the *key* instrument—that the Lord had used to draw them to saving faith.

On one Sunday, during the announcements before the morning service had begun, I decided to demonstrate this very thing to the congregation. I asked each person in the room to stand who would say that the Lord had used Simon as the key person in their life to bring them to saving faith. Eight to ten of the older men of the congregation stood. I then asked everyone to look at these men, many of whom were ordained elders in the church, and asked those to stand who would say that the Lord had used one of *these* men as the principal individual in their own lives who had drawn them to saving faith. At this point, a third of the room stood. Then came an incredible sight I will never forget. I asked everyone to look at these individuals who were now standing and to stand, as well, if the Lord had employed any of these faithful saints to be the primary individuals who had led *them* to saving faith. In a congregation that numbered around four hundred people, maybe forty people remained sitting that Sunday morning.

Simon took the congregation's baptismal vow seriously.[3] He understood that children were members of the covenant community and were worth ministering to. In fact, he went out of his way to minister to them. By all accounts, Simon was a man of average talents—but the Lord used him in a mighty way. You don't need to possess ten talents. You don't need to have nine. You simply need to be faithful with what the Lord has given you, in the context where he has placed you, and with the people who are before you. Our God does mighty things with weak vessels.

The Blessing of the Reminder

When we witness a baptism as part of our community life, we are reminded that God calls us, as the church, to live in a way that is distinct from the world. Baptism serves as a visible reminder that God has set us apart. In 1 Corinthians 10:1–7, Paul writes,

> For I do not want you to be unaware, brothers, that our fathers were all under the cloud, and all passed through the sea, and all were baptized into Moses in the cloud and in the sea, and all ate the same spiritual food, and all drank the same spiritual drink. For they drank from the spiritual Rock that followed them, and the Rock was Christ. Nevertheless, with most of them God was not pleased, for they were overthrown in the wilderness.
>
> Now these things took place as examples for us, that we might not desire evil as they did. Do not be idolaters as some of them were.

Paul points the Corinthian church to the Israelites and the Red Sea. He wants the Corinthians to learn from the fact that, while the entire nation of Israel was "baptized" while taking part in the exodus, not all of them avoided falling into idolatry and judgment. The Lord called them forth from the world, and yet they became like the world. Baptism serves as a visible reminder that a calling has been placed on our lives. We are part of a distinct community—one that belongs to the sovereign, living God. We are set apart, but we must continue to live in light of our baptism.

The writer of Hebrews issues a warning along the same lines: "For good news came to us just as to them, but the message they heard did not benefit them, because they were not united by faith with those who listened" (Heb. 4:2). And J. V. Fesko comments, "As with Israel of old, therefore, baptism places a boundary and marks the covenant community off from the unbelieving world, but the community that is marked is the *visible* community. Just as with ancient Israel, faith and disbelief are the all-determining factors in whether baptism is received as covenant blessing or sanction."[4] Baptism reminds us to be a community that lives differently and distinctly from those who are outside our community. Our baptism serves as a blessing to us if we receive Christ and the promises that he has signified through it—but if we do not, the greater judgment will be ours.

The Blessing of Solidarity

Evangelicals place an emphasis upon personal conversion, which is a right and necessary emphasis, but we often lose sight of the communal nature of our faith. The entire community is marked, by baptism, as belonging not only to God but also to one another. And this has always been true for the people of God: in Abraham's day, everyone who joined the house of Abraham—even a person who came from a pagan culture—was no longer considered to be an outsider but now considered to be part of the community. The members of his household belonged first and foremost to one another. There was solidarity among them.

When we witness a baptism, we see an illustration of the church's solidarity. Circumcision provided this same illustration—when Abraham received the sign of the covenant, his entire house was circumcised: Ishmael (a thirteen-year-old) as well as all the other men who were born into his house and even all the foreigners who were brought into it. Abraham was saved both unto God and into community—and we see the same in the New Testament: when God showers us with his grace, he saves us unto himself as well as unto one another. The unity of the people of God is a reality.

Paul says in Ephesians 4:4–6,

> There is one body and one Spirit—just as you were called to the one hope that belongs to your call—one Lord, one faith, one baptism, one God and Father of all, who is over all and through all and in all.

Baptism proclaims our union. And, as John Murray rightfully states, "It is because believers are united to Christ in the efficacy of his death, in the power of his resurrection, and in the fellowship of his grace that they are one body."[5] We live our Christian faith in community. I often tell the congregation that I serve, "I need you, and you need me. I need your love, your sacrificial giving, your service, your spiritual gifts, your encouragement, your prayers. And you need mine." There is no Lone Ranger Christianity. There is not even a Lone Ranger and Tonto Christianity.

We need and belong to one another. And baptism signifies and reminds the church of this blessing.

The Blessing of Their Example

In chapter 3 we considered the value that children have in the eyes of Christ. And he also sets children before our eyes as a model. Jesus calls a child to himself in Matthew 18 and, as he places the child in the middle of them, tells his disciples, "Whoever humbles himself like this child is the greatest in the kingdom of heaven" (v. 4). Small children offer us a picture of utter trust and reliance—of simple, unadorned, trusting faith. And we need their example. When covenantal baptism takes place within our community, it reminds us not to look past these members of our family.

I remember well that when I would walk into a store or enter a crowd with my children when they were younger, I could simply lower my hand and stretch it backward, and a little hand would embrace my hand. My children would follow where I led—that was trust.

Jesus desires for us, as children of God, to look to the Father in trusting faith the same way that a little child depends on his or her parents. The more we mature in the faith, the more our own lived-out faith looks like that of a child: simple, dependent, utter trust. We have much to learn from children—all of us. And so a congregation is blessed by witnessing the baptism of small children.

That baptism pictures before us our own helplessness, our utter dependence, our call to simple trusting faith, and God's great grace.

The Blessing of the Reminder to Improve Our Own Baptisms

Each time we witness a public baptism, we are encouraged by God to reflect on our own baptisms. Reformed theology has long maintained that baptism benefits the one who receives it for the entire course of his or her life. That is why question 167 of the Westminster Larger Catechism asks, "How is our baptism to be improved by us?" And, as we saw in chapter 3, we all have the opportunity to improve our own baptisms. As Sinclair Ferguson helpfully states, "Baptism is the rubric under which the entire liturgy of the Christian life is expressed."[6] Our baptism points to our union with Christ and reassures us of the hope we have in our covenant-keeping God. It does this while also exhorting us to live a life of thanksgiving to the Lord and to seek to put off our body of sinful flesh and walk in righteousness. And we enjoy this "liturgy of the Christian life" as we live in union not only with our Savior but also with the people of God—since, as we have seen, we have been saved unto God and unto one another. What a wonderful sign and seal of our salvation the Lord has gifted to his people. Baptism occurs in a moment, but its reverberations sound throughout a person's entire life.

May we not only look back to our baptisms but continue to live in them going forward.

Conclusion

As we baptize our covenant children in the midst of the covenant community, blessings flow to that entire community. Baptism is a community sacrament. God graciously provided this sign and seal of his covenant not only for the individual but for the body. May we rejoice at his kindness each and every time we witness the baptism of a child in the church.

Questions for Further Reflection

1. What makes baptism a congregational sacrament?
2. What are some ways you could assist the parents in your congregation with the Christian nurture of their children?
3. How does baptism mark the church as being a visible community?
4. What are some particular ways that you might "improve" on your own baptism?
5. After reading through this book, how would you articulate the blessings of baptism and the kindness God has shown by gifting it to his people?

QUESTIONS AND ANSWERS
ON BAPTISM

In the following pages you will find questions with short answers—at least, answers as short as I could muster. Baptism raises a myriad of questions from various quarters. I can't answer every question that every person might raise about baptism, so I have included a list of recommended resources at the end of this book for further reading.

Circumcision was administered only to male children in Israel—so, if baptism is circumcision's New Testament counterpart, why are both male and female children baptized? Isn't this a strike against the argument for continuity?

All branches of the Christian church recognize that there is both continuity and discontinuity between the old covenant and the new covenant. The very fact that we baptize instead of circumcise is an example of this discontinuity. However, the continuity of the covenant of grace, as we discussed in chapter 1, proves dominant. It is not surprising that girls are now included in the receiving of the covenant sign. The new covenant establishes a more inclusive, free, and gracious era, and we should expect to see its sacrament of initiation become more inclusive, not less. This, in fact, remains one of the greatest issues with the baptistic view. Its doctrine of church membership and baptism presents the new covenant era as actually being more restrictive than the old covenant era.

Wasn't circumcision an identification of an individual's citizenship rather than of his belonging to the "church"?

The Jewish people held the unique position of being both the covenant people of God as well as a nation—they existed as both a church and a state. We often think of these two realms as being separated. However, Israel was a theocracy; for it, the separation between church and state did not exist. A child who was born into the covenant community was recognized as a member of both the state and the church. As we noted in chapter 1, God gave the gift of circumcision to be a sacrament of the covenant of grace. It surely identified those who belonged to the nation, but it was commanded because of the significance of its function as a spiritual mark of those who belonged to the covenant people of God (i.e., the church).

Are children of believers automatically saved?

No. Neither birth nor baptism secures salvation for our children, any more than Ishmael's birth and circumcision secured salvation for him. Salvation is by grace alone through faith alone in Christ alone. Covenant children must possess a personal faith in Christ Jesus—one that involves knowledge, assent, and trust—in order to be saved. Therefore, we should continually point them to Christ by teaching them the Scriptures, reminding them of their baptism, praying with and for them, modeling faith in Christ before them, and participating with them in the corporate worship of the church. They themselves must believe—and if, in fact, they continue in unbelief, they will reap the sanctions that are attached to covenant unfaithfulness. Isaac received the blessing, while Ishmael received the condemnation. God's normative way of working, though, is to bring covenant children to saving faith in Christ.

Wouldn't it be consistent to practice paedocommunion along with infant baptism?

No. While God commanded that children receive the sign of circumcision, he gave no command to include children in the Passover meal. The Old Testament contains commands for them to be included in the Feast of Weeks and the Feast of Booths, but no such command exists regarding the Passover. In fact, we might contend that a passage like Luke 2:42, in which we see Jesus going to

Jerusalem to celebrate the feast at the age of twelve, implies that younger children were excluded from participating.

Even more importantly, Paul warns us against taking the Lord's Table without self-examination. A participant must be able to "discern the body," lest he or she eat or drink judgment upon himself or herself (see 1 Cor. 11:27–32). Neither children nor adults should take communion until they have professed faith and been admitted to the Table by elders of the church. And small children cannot discern the difference between the Lord's Table and snack time. They cannot, and will not, understand that communion is a remembrance of Christ's death. They cannot understand that the bread represents Christ's body, nor will they comprehend their obligation to others in the church body. They will not be able to examine themselves. And those who come to the Table unworthily, irreverently, or ignorantly defame what it signifies. Paul talks about people who became sick and even fell asleep—in other words, died—as a result of taking the Table in such a manner (see 1 Cor. 11:30). When we make this sacrament something it isn't by giving it to our children before they make a profession of faith, we lead them into the way of not grace but judgment.

Is the baptism that John administered the same as the one that we practice?

The baptism that John the Baptist administered to individuals differs significantly from the baptism that

Jesus commands his disciples to observe. Luke makes a sharp distinction between them in Acts 18:25, as does Paul in Acts 19:3–5. John's baptism prepared the way for the coming of the Messiah. Therefore, its meaning "was rooted and grounded in the Old Testament,"[1] as the late Reformed teacher R.C. Sproul wrote. It served as a baptism of repentance and provided a transition from the old to the new in anticipation of the Messiah to come.

Why was Jesus baptized, then?

Jesus, as the perfect man, had no need for a baptism of repentance. However, in order to identify with his people and "fulfill all righteousness" (Matt. 3:15), he willingly underwent the waters of baptism. By speaking that phrase, Jesus was alluding to Isaiah 53—the famous text on the Suffering Servant, which says, "by his knowledge shall the righteous one, my servant, make many to be accounted righteous, and he shall bear their iniquities" (v. 11). Jesus, our Lord, is the Suffering Servant who came to identify with his people and to bear our iniquities so that we might be counted righteous. Picture the long line of people who are being baptized by John. Jesus, the Christ, approaches them. He has every right to condemn them all. But instead he enters the line and says, "Let me be baptized as they are baptized and be counted among them."

The water baptism that Jesus received from John pointed forward to the baptism in blood that he would experience upon the cross for his people. "In his death and resurrection the core significance of both his circumcision and his baptism, and therefore of Abraham's circumcision and of our baptism, meet."[2] Circumcision and baptism both point to the atoning death he died upon the cross for sinners.

Does baptism cause regeneration?

Paul explains in 1 Corinthians 1:17 that Christ sent him to preach the gospel, not to baptize. If baptism were the primary converting means of grace, then Paul *would* have been sent to baptize—or at least to preach the gospel and baptize together. Yet he states that God sent him to preach the gospel only. The Word and the sacraments, while they work together, must also be differentiated. The sacraments, including baptism, primarily serve to strengthen faith, whereas God uses the Word for that purpose as well as for regeneration and implanting faith in the first place.

Doesn't baptizing children imply that you think they are, or will be, regenerate?

No. We neither presume nor infer regeneration by baptism. Could an infant child be regenerated? Yes—the Spirit blows where he wills (see John 3:8), and in Luke 1:41 John the Baptist shows signs of regeneration while he is in his mother's womb! God wills and works as he pleases—but we are not making any assertion about God's regenerating work in a child whom we baptize. The baptism of a covenant child recognizes that child's entrance into the visible church, but it makes no statement regarding his or her entrance into the invisible church.

Does infant baptism declare that you know what is happening in the heart of a child who is baptized?

None of us know a person's heart, and we do not presume to know the baptized child's heart. Yet baptism does involve some level of presumption. As B. B. Warfield, a great nineteenth-century Reformed scholar, stated, "All baptism is inevitably administered on the basis not of knowledge but of presumption. And if we must baptize on presumption, the whole principle is yielded; and it would seem that we must baptize all whom we may fairly presume to be members of Christ's body."[3] The baptistic view presumes upon the confession of an adult—that his or her confession is real and true. Covenantal baptism presumes not upon an individual's promise but on God's covenantal promises. As Warfield goes on to say, "Assuredly a human profession is no more solid basis to build upon than a Divine promise. So soon, therefore, as it is fairly apprehended that we baptize on presumption and not on knowledge, it is inevitable that we shall baptize all those for whom we may, on any grounds, fairly cherish a good presumption that they belong to God's people—and this surely includes the infant children of believers."[4]

Does baptizing our covenant children speak to our expectations or hope for them?

Absolutely. The seventeenth-century Dutch theologian Johannes Cocceius's commentary on question 74 of the Heidelberg Catechism stated that baptism "signifies not merely that there is an external sanctity arising from their not being conceived and born like heathen children … but also that there is good reason to hope that they may really be sanctified from their tender years so that when they reach the years of understanding, they will through God's blessing upon the instructions of their parents discern and love the truth."[5] By hearing the Word and being prayed for, these covenant children are continually being put in the way of God's grace, and so we expect and hope that they will believe. Our covenant children are truly privileged, among all the children in the world, and so we have great hope for them.

If baptism doesn't save, is there any comfort for Christian parents in the baptism of an infant who later dies?

Although baptism doesn't save, its waters signify the promises of our covenant-keeping God—and his covenantal promises are for both us and our children. The kindness and graciousness that we see in our heavenly Father should give us confidence that our children who die in infancy are indeed with him. As Cocceius stated, "if they should die in infancy, then, as holy persons and members of Christ, they shall be saved. All this we believe on the ground of the promise given to Abraham, and through him to all believers, that Jehovah would be the God—that is, the sanctifier and the justifier—not of him only but also of his seed."[6] David's story from 2 Samuel 12:15–23 reinforces the fact that we can have this confidence. The sin that David commits with Bathsheba incurs judgement from the Lord. Part of this judgment involves the sickness and eventual death of the infant child who is born to David from this illicit union. David spends seven days fasting and pleading with God for the life of his child. When his servants inform him, on the seventh day, that his child has died, he arises, washes, anoints himself, changes clothes, and goes to the house of the Lord to worship. His servants ask why he fasted and wept while the child was sick but then worshipped when he died. David's response is "While the child was still alive, I fasted and wept, for I said, 'Who knows whether the LORD will be gracious to me, that the child may live?' But now he is dead. Why should I fast? Can I bring him back again? I shall go to him, but he will not return to me." David believes that he "shall go to" his child. If he simply means that he will die and be buried the way that his son has died and been buried, then there is no reason for joy or comfort. Rather, he arises in peace with the knowledge that he will be reunited with his son in glory. The baptism of a child, though it doesn't save, points to promises God has made that should comfort a parent's soul by bringing confidence and hope.

Are the sacraments necessary for salvation?

No; they are not absolutely necessary for salvation—but God commands them, and so we are obliged to participate in them (even though they are more than an obligation; they are gifts God has given to us). If we neglect the sacraments, we experience spiritual deprivation—doing so has effects, just as persistently disobeying God in *any* respect will have effects on the spiritual life. We know, however, that the sacraments are not *necessary* for salvation. Berkhof, a Reformed systematic theologian, makes these points:

1. From the free spiritual character of the gospel dispensation, in which God does not bind His grace to the use of certain external forms (Luke 18:14; John 4:21–23).

2. From the fact that Scripture mentions only faith as the instrumental condition of salvation (John 3:36; 5:24; 6:29; Acts 16:31).

3. From the fact that the sacraments do not originate faith but presuppose it, and are administered where faith is assumed (Acts 2:41; 16:14, 15, 30, 33; 1 Cor. 11:23–32)

4. From the fact that many were actually saved without the use of the sacraments. Think of the believers before the time of Abraham and of the penitent thief on the cross.[7]

If baptism itself does not save and isn't a requirement for salvation, why do Scripture passages such as Mark 16:16; Acts 2:38; and 1 Peter 3:21 seem to say that it does and is?

Verses such as these employ what theologians call sacramental language—language in which a sign can stand for the thing it is signifying. Genesis 17:10; Acts 22:16; and 1 Corinthians 5:7 all contain additional examples of this. In Genesis 17:10, God describes his covenant in terms of circumcision. In Acts 22:16, baptism is equated with the washing away of sins. And 1 Corinthians 5:7 calls Christ the Passover Lamb. Such a close relationship can exist between a sign and the thing it is signifying that, at times, the Scriptures will use them interchangeably.

My covenant children have not believed. Does this mean that I have failed? Or that the covenant promises of God have failed?

Neither. Our adversary loves to sow the seeds of guilt and doubt—those are two of his greatest weapons. I have no doubt that you were not a perfect parent; no parents are. Nor did you model the faith perfectly; no parent has. But if you are a Christian parent, I'm confident that you pointed your children to Christ and taught them about him. So now you must rest upon his promises—and God provides great rest for Christian parents. He does not turn a blind eye or a deaf ear to his children—and you are his child. He is a covenant-keeping God, and we can pray for our children with confidence, because he works according to his covenant promises. So pray the promises of God for your children. They have heard the Word, their baptism calls out to them, "Believe, believe, believe," and they have been pointed to the faith by the example you have set through the years. Salvation is all of God and wholly his work, and baptism is a good reminder of this—one that we often need. So pray with confidence that he will make your children his children.

The only believers whom we see receiving baptism in the New Testament are adults. Doesn't it seem odd that, if infant baptism is allowable, none of the believers we see in the Gospels and in Acts had received covenantal baptism?

We should expect to see adult baptisms in the Gospels—in fact, it would have been impossible for a covenantal baptism to have taken place during that time. Why? Because no individuals could have been born into a Christian home during the time of the Gospels. And we should expect to see the same thing in the book of Acts. We are witnessing the first generation of Christians within the Gospels and Acts, so of course these first converts received baptism upon making a profession of faith. As Geoffrey Bromily points out, "The first baptisms in the New Testament are parallel to the first circumcisions in the Old Testament."[8] Furthermore, in the case of Lydia, her entire household is baptized when she comes to saving faith (see Acts 16:15). We cannot assert that children were definitely included in that instance of baptism; but Luke goes out of his way to make it clear that upon her profession of faith, her entire household was baptized.

Fesko helpfully speaks to this issue when he says, "Baptists contend that a profession of faith is the administrative ground for baptism; only those who make a profession of faith receive the rite. They base this argument on what they see in the New Testament narratives that recount the baptisms of converts to the Christian faith. However, this argument rests on only half of the canon and fails once again to account for the doctrine of the covenant."[9] Should covenant children, who have always been considered as being among the people of God, continue to receive the sacrament of initiation into his covenant people—or did something change regarding the status of these children as a result of the move from the old covenant to the new covenant? That is the central question for us to ask as we consider the entire Scriptures.

In Acts 2:38, when Peter is preaching during Pentecost, he commands his listeners, "Repent and be baptized." Infants cannot repent—so how can they be baptized?

The word "and" in this verse functions as a coordinating conjunction, not a causal conjunction. That is to say, the "repent[ing]" does not *cause* the "be[ing] baptized."

Neither does the word indicate a logical order for these commands—as if a person who has first repented should then be baptized. Rather, these are two equally important commands. Note, as well, that the conjunction "for" at the beginning of the following verse links it with this one—verse 38 cannot be understood apart from verse 39. The fact that "the promise is for you and for your children and for all who are far off, everyone whom the Lord our God calls to himself" provides the grounds for the commands to "repent" and "be baptized" that we see in verse 38. It is those who receive God's promises who are to be baptized—and in verse 39 Peter includes covenant children within that number.

It has been stated that baptism is a sign and a seal of the saving work Christ has done to fulfill the covenant of grace. Since it is a seal, shouldn't a person receive baptism after already having faith?

The promises that baptism represents, signifies, and seals are not tied to the moment when baptism is administered. Upon receiving the sacrament in infancy or childhood, an individual may see these promises realized in his or her life at eight days old, eight years old, or eighty-eight years old. Furthermore, as chapter 1 discussed, baptism serves primarily as a seal not of a person's subjective faith but of God's faithfulness. What it principally seals is God's promises, not our own.

If baptism means "to immerse," isn't that an argument against baptizing infants?

The Eastern Orthodox Church has historically baptized infants by immersion. In fact, historical records testify that they were baptizing infants by a triple immersion as early as the eighth century.[10] Therefore, we want to be careful about making the assertion that any particular mode of baptism (e.g., immersion) rules out any particular subjects of the baptism (e.g., infants).

Does the word for baptism in the New Testament always mean "to immerse"?

The word that the New Testament uses for baptism—baptizo, in its various forms—can mean "to immerse," but that isn't necessarily how it should always be defined. If indeed baptism requires that immersion be performed, then we would expect the word that the Bible uses for baptism to always mean to immerse—and yet that is far from the case. It is used various ways in the New Testament, and in writings outside the New Testament as well.

For example, the author of Hebrews mentions the various "washings" (*baptismois*) that were performed in the Old Testament (Heb. 9:10). These washings included "the sprinkling of defiled persons" (v. 13) and the account of when Moses "took the blood of calves and goats, with water and scarlet wool and hyssop, and sprinkled both the book itself and all the people" (v. 19). The chapter goes on to detail one more of these "washings":

the time when blood was "sprinkled [on] both the tent and all the vessels used in worship" (v. 21). The writer of Hebrews considers these to be examples of the same kind of "washings" that the word for *baptism* indicates—and they are all instances of something being *sprinkled*.

In Mark 7, Jesus's disciples are criticized for not washing their hands before they eat. We are informed in verse 3 that the Pharisees and the Jews did not eat unless they would "*baptisontai.*" In verse 4, Mark relays other rules that the Pharisees observed, including the "washings" (*baptismous*) of dining couches. And the Pharisees here are clearly not immersing themselves or their dining couches.

In 1 Corinthians 10:2, Paul, after referencing the crossing of the Red Sea, says that "all were baptized [*ebaptisanto*] into Moses in the cloud and in the sea." The point of this passage is consecration. No one would contend that the Israelites were "immersed" in the sea—the Egyptians were! The Israelites were, at best, sprinkled by it.

Luke 11:38 will suffice as our final example of how this word is used. Luke comments that a Pharisee "was astonished to see that [Jesus] did not first wash before dinner." The word that is translated "wash" here is again a form of *baptizo*. Clearly what astonished this Pharisee was not that Christ didn't *immerse* himself before eating.

There are clearly times when the writers of the New Testament use this term to refer to a mode other than immersion. Therefore, it cannot be contended that *baptizo* indicates that baptism *must* be by immersion, because the word doesn't always mean to immerse; it contains a range of meanings. So while the argument can be made that immersion is a valid form of baptism,[11] it is not the required form.

Is immersion allowable?

Yes. Immersion serves as a fine mode of baptism. The mode of baptizing itself is not essential—though most people in the history of Reformed theology have argued that pouring or sprinkling better signifies the meaning and purpose of baptism.

Why baptize by pouring or sprinkling?

If any baptism that occurs in the New Testament proves important as a precedent for pouring or sprinkling, surely it is the baptism at Pentecost described in Acts 2. This is the baptism that Joel prophesied (see Joel 2:28–29), that John pointed to (see Matt. 3:11–12), and that Christ promised would come (see Acts 1:5; 11:16)—both John and Jesus outright calling it a baptism as they did so. And what occurs during that baptism? The Spirit is poured out. Since baptism signifies that pouring out of the Spirit, a pouring or sprinkling of the water does this most accurately. Presbyterians also sprinkle because baptism signifies the fact that we have been cleansed by the blood of the Lamb. On the great Day of Atonement each year, the high priest would sprinkle the blood from Israel's sin offerings onto the mercy seat (see Lev.

16:14–15). This provided atonement for the people of God—and also pointed forward to the atoning work that Christ would perform as the Lamb of God. Baptism now points back to this atoning work, and sprinkling provides a strong visual of this.

But what about the references we see in the New Testament to baptized individuals going "into" the water? Doesn't that prove that baptism is done through immersion?

The Greek preposition that we're talking about here—*eis*—has a range of meanings. It surely can mean "into," but it can also mean "to," "toward," "unto," "for," and "among." For example, this one preposition occurs eleven times throughout Acts 8—and English Bibles translate those eleven occurrences in various ways. In the ESV we find the word translated as "to" seven times (vv. 3, 5, 20, 25, 26, 27, 40), "at" one time (v. 40), "in" twice (vv. 16, 23), and "into" (v. 38) only once.

The way that both this word and *baptizo* are invoked indicate how, more often than not, the argument for baptism by immersion tends to employ circular reasoning. When the word for *baptism* is examined, we are often told that it means "to immerse" because the circumstances in which the Bible uses it make it clear that this is what is occurring. But when this circumstantial evidence is examined, and it is demonstrated that there is no proof that people are described as going "into" the water (as is argued from the use of this preposition as well), then it is maintained that this must have occurred because that is what *baptizo* means.

Doesn't the case of the Ethiopian eunuch point to baptism by immersion?

There is no evidence to support such a conclusion—in fact, the circumstantial evidence points in the opposite direction. The Ethiopian eunuch is said to be traveling in a "desert place" (Acts 8:26). The place the account is describing is the barren region of the Negev, south of Judea. Finding enough water there to immerse someone seems unlikely at best.

When the eunuch and Philip come to water, the eunuch cries out to be baptized. It is safe to assume that Philip has explained baptism to him by this point—but from where has the eunuch drawn the conclusion that he should be baptized in the first place? The eunuch was reading from the book of Isaiah when Philip found him, and he had been reading for a period of time—long enough to wrestle with the text. In the vicinity of the passage that we know he was reading (see Acts 8:32–33), we find the line "So shall he sprinkle many nations" (Isa. 52:15). This is the only reference to water in the surrounding text from Isaiah.

The fact that the text says they then went "into" and "out of" the water does not imply immersion. As John Murray says,

It should be noted that Philip as well as the eunuch went down into the water and came up out of the water. If such expressions imply or prove immersion, then they mean that Philip immersed himself as well as the eunuch. . . .

The expressions, "they both went down into the water" and "they came up out of the water" are satisfied by the thought that they both went down to the water, stood on the brink or stepped into the edge, and that Philip baptised the eunuch by scooping up the water and pouring it or sprinkling it on him.[12]

Could Philip have immersed him? Yes; but the text neither demands nor proves that contention. We don't know the actual mode of baptism that Philip employed here, so this text does not support a baptistic argument.

What about the baptism Paul receives in Acts?

The account of Paul's baptism also hints that immersion did not take place. He is in the house of Judas when God sends Ananias to him, and in Acts 9:17 we are told that Ananias "entered the house." After he informs Paul that has God sent him, we read, "And immediately something like scales fell from his eyes, and he regained his sight. Then he rose and was baptized; and taking food, he was strengthened" (vv. 18–19). In both of the accounts we are given of this event—Acts 9 as well as Acts 22—the narrative moves quickly; it appears that Paul simply rises and receives baptism. The most straightforward reading of these texts implies that he does not leave the home; and it is doubtful, at the very least, that a house possessed the means for him to be immersed. Therefore, even the apostle Paul's own baptism account suggests that he was baptized via sprinkling or pouring rather than by immersion.

What about the Philippian jailer's baptism?

The baptism that Paul and Silas performed on the Philippian jailer and his household occurred after the two apostles had been scourged and beaten by their captors. It would have been a difficult task for these two wearied evangelists, after surviving such a night, to have then baptized an entire family by immersion. Since the jail would not have contained sufficient water for baptism by immersion, baptizing this family between midnight and sunrise would have required the herculean task of departing the jail, winding their way down to a riverside in the dark, and there immersing an entire family. And all this after they had received a severe beating!

The more likely sequence of events is that, after the Philippian jailer "brought them out" (Acts 16:30) from the "inner prison" (v. 24), he and his family received baptism in the larger portion of the jail—which also contained his house (see v. 34)—by way of sprinkling or pouring. Further evidence for this view presents itself when we consider how Paul refused to exit the jail, once the magistrates ordered him and Silas to leave, and required the magistrates to come and lead them out instead (see v. 37).

Would they have left the jail in the middle of the night, without the consent of the magistrates, only for Paul to require them to come in and let him and Silas go after they did have the magistrates' consent? It would have undermined his entire position and argument if he had done so.

But wasn't the "baptism" of the Spirit a type of immersion, since Acts 2:2 says that "it filled the entire house"?

This account from Acts doesn't say that the *Spirit* "filled the entire house." The Spirit is first mentioned *after* this has happened, in verses 3 and 4. The closest antecedent to the "it" that verse 2 says filled the house is the "sound" that this phrase is actually referring to: "And suddenly there came from heaven a sound like a mighty rushing wind, and it filled the entire house where they were sitting." It's only afterward that we read about the way in which the Spirit descended on the apostles: "Divided tongues as of fire appeared to them and rested on each one of them" (Acts 2:3). No doubt this "sound" is tied to the Spirit, but it is the "sound" itself, not the Spirit, that fills the house.

In Romans 6, Paul says we were "buried" with Christ through baptism and then "raised" with him. Doesn't immersion best symbolize that process?

Romans 6 is not about the mode of baptism; rather, it is addressing our identification with Christ. This passage is better understood as referring not to water baptism but rather to the fact that our identity changes as we are "immersed" in Christ. The term used for "baptism" in the New Testament world denoted some sort of change taking place. Josephus, the first-century Jewish historian, used it of crowds that flooded (or *baptized*) Jerusalem and "wrecked the city."[13] Jesus uses the term to indicate a transformation when he speaks of his death as a baptism in Mark 10:38 and Luke 12:50. Paul employs it to denote the same thing. Two examples will suffice to demonstrate this. In 1 Corinthians 10:2, he recalls how the Israelites "were baptized into Moses in the cloud and in the sea"— referring to the Red Sea crossing. Yet when the Israelites made that crossing, they were not immersed in water but rather joined to Moses and identified with him on the basis of not being able to return to Egypt. And Paul uses the term again in Galatians 3:27, in which he makes the point that being baptized into Christ means being united with him.

Furthermore, the perception that immersion symbolizes our dying and rising with Christ springs more from our Western practice of burial than from Christ's actual burial. He was not buried in the ground; he was buried in a cave in the side of a hill. His rising was not so much a case of "Up from the grave he arose" as "Out from the grave he arose."

Is covenantal baptism a holdover of Roman Catholicism?

Covenantal baptism does not present the sacraments as possessing power in and of themselves, the way the

Roman Catholic Church teaches. Roman Catholicism teaches that the sacraments, including baptism, are effective *ex opere operato* ("from the work performed")—in other words, that there is an efficacy in the doing that makes them necessary for regeneration. The Reformed tradition rejects such a view; it maintains, rather, that the sacraments have power and are efficacious (i.e., effective) only through the Holy Spirit and according to his working[14] as they are embraced solely by faith. In a quote that was referenced earlier in the book, Calvin nicely illustrates why we need to have faith when we receive the sacraments: "They avail and profit nothing unless received in faith. As with wine or oil or some other liquid, no matter how much you pour out, it will flow away and disappear unless the mouth of the vessel to receive it is open; moreover, the vessel will be splashed over on the outside, but will still remain void and empty."[15]

Does the act of baptism make children into members of the church?

Covenant children receive baptism as a sign that they are already counted as members of the visible church. They enter into the covenant community upon conception, and thus they are entitled to receive the sign of entrance into that community as soon as they are able to. Baptism does not cause this membership but rather signifies it.

How old is too old for a covenant child to be baptized? At what age should a profession of faith be required before a person is baptized?

Leaders in different churches may come to different conclusions regarding this question, and it is best answered by your local elders. However, a good principle to bring to bear is that as long as a child is not yet considered to be a young adult, he or she may rightly receive baptism as a covenantal child. If a child shows resistance to being baptized and is of a sufficient age to articulate a lack of belief, then he or she should not be baptized.

Is there an age of accountability?

The idea of an age of accountability arose during the nineteenth and early twentieth centuries among Protestants from an Arminian tradition who were trying to explain what happens to children who die in infancy. The Arminian view has no covenantal promises to offer to covenant children. Therefore, to alleviate the grief of covenant children being relegated to hell in their theological system, these Arminians developed the idea of the age of accountability. But no such notion can be found in the Scriptures—we see that we are all held accountable from the time of our conception.

Clearly we each reach an age when we begin to comprehend the faith in a more mature way; but this will develop differently across different children, and thus establishing an arbitrary age makes little sense. Some children will understand the faith earlier than others, and all need to hear the free offer of the gospel regardless of their age. Therefore, we ought to appeal to our children, from their earliest days, to believe and embrace the covenant promises that have been made to them.[16]

Why are children baptized into the visible church when they may prove to be unregenerate? Doesn't Jeremiah 31:31–34 make it clear that all God's people will know him? And thus, isn't the church no longer a mixed community of the regenerate and the unregenerate, as it was under the old covenant?

The promises regarding the new covenant that are found in this passage have, as is true of much of the new covenant, been inaugurated but not yet consummated. They fall under the theological category that is commonly recognized as "already but not yet." All Christians recognize that this dynamic exists in the present, because all of us still evangelize. None of us believe that we currently exist in a state in which "no longer shall each one teach his neighbor and each his brother, saying, 'Know the LORD,' for they shall all know me, from the least of them to the greatest" (Jer. 31:34). We still await the return of Christ so that this will be fully consummated. Some Christians, however, still argue that the new covenant differs from the old covenant in that the new covenant community is a regenerate community.

In contrast, Reformed theology distinguishes between the visible and the invisible church. There are some members of the visible church (the community that *professes* belief in the Lord Jesus Christ) who will prove not to be members of the invisible church (the community of all *true* believers of all ages and in all places). Not all who are baptized into the visible church—whether as adults or as children—will necessarily be saved. The church isn't a fully regenerate community. For some people, baptism will be—as was circumcision in the Old Testament—a sign of judgment.

As Fesko points out, the contrast that we witness in Jeremiah 31:31–34 "is not between the new covenant and the Abrahamic covenant, but between the new and old covenant (the Mosaic covenant). Verse 32 clearly states that the new covenant would not be like the covenant that God made with the fathers when He brought them out of Egypt."[17] Furthermore, even in this text, God makes the promise with covenant children in view (see Jer. 32:38–41), which continues the idea of the Abrahamic Covenant. As Fesko asserts, "This means that the new covenant is organically connected to the Abrahamic covenant and that the Mosaic covenant expires."[18] The new covenant community remains, in this present age, a mixed community of regenerate and unregenerate individuals. One day the invisible church will be revealed, and in it there will be no mixture—but until that happens, at the return of Christ, the visible church will always be mixed.

Isn't it sufficient to say that children *can* be baptized? Do we need to say they *should* be baptized?

If God considers children to be members of the covenant community, then neglecting covenantal baptism means we are keeping one of the chief means of God's grace from our covenant children's lives. This would be a serious error.

Should people who were baptized in the Roman Catholic Church be baptized again?

To be fair, the answer to this question has not been uniform throughout Reformed church history. Yet most of the Reformed tradition has understood Roman Catholic baptism to be a legitimate type of baptism (though there was a significant portion of the American Presbyterian church, before the American Civil War, that argued otherwise). Most of the magisterial Reformers (e.g., Luther, Zwingli, Melanchthon, and so on) were baptized within the Roman church, so this was not a small issue. And as they acknowledged, and as we must remember, there is only one baptism (see Eph. 4:5). And the efficacy of that baptism is not tied to the person who administers it. Rather, a baptism that is administered with water, in the name of the Trinity, and with the intent of signifying Christ and his benefits is a valid baptism. Charles Hodge, who argued strongly on the side of the validity of Roman baptism, stated, "The error of the Romanists concerning the absolute necessity and uniform efficacy (in the case of infants) of baptism, is very great, but it cannot invalidate the nature of the ordinance."[19]

What if I was "baptized" in a Mormon, Jesus-Only Pentecostal, or Jehovah's Witness church?

You should approach the elders and pastor of the church you attend and ask to be baptized. Baptisms that are performed in any of these contexts are done so outside the sphere of Christian baptism. These traditions deny the basic tenets of Christianity, as detailed by the historic creeds of the church, and thus lie outside the bounds of the Christian faith.

Is it wrong to be baptized again, as a believer, if someone was baptized as an infant? What if I simply want to make a public profession of my faith?

Yes, it is wrong—because there is only one baptism (see Eph. 4:5). We call the purpose of baptism into question when we receive it more than once. Baptism is based not upon the individual but upon the working of the Spirit and the covenant promises God has made to us in Christ Jesus. Being "baptized again" is an impossibility. A desire to make a public profession of faith is commendable. However, becoming a communing member of the church, attending corporate worship weekly, and living one's life as a "living sacrifice" unto God constitutes a public profession on its own (Rom. 12:1; see also v. 2).

Should we allow anyone to administer baptism?

The sacraments, by their very nature, serve as a visible sign of what is proclaimed in the Word of God. The Word governs the sacraments, and therefore it would be improper to observe them in a context in which the Word is not preached. Paul asserts that ministers are "stewards of the mysteries of God" (1 Cor. 4:1)—and thus, since the administration of the sacraments has, for most of Reformed church history, been understood as an extension of the preached Word, it has been reserved for teaching elders or pastors alone.

What if I was baptized by a non-pastor, such as a fellow teenager, my father, my mother, an aunt, a camp counselor, or a university campus ministry worker?

Though the previous answer stands, the efficacy of baptism does not depend on the one who is administering it. As the Westminster Larger Catechism says, "The sacraments become effectual means of salvation, not by any power in themselves, or any virtue derived from the piety or intention of him by whom they are administered, but only by the working of the Holy Ghost, and the blessing of Christ, by whom they are instituted."[20] Even if it is not administered by an ordained pastor, a baptism that is administered with water in the triune name of God can be a true baptism.

Let us, however, remind ourselves that baptism serves as a sign of an individual's entrance into the visible church. The sacraments are not simply individualistic acts of private piety; baptism was given to the visible church and is therefore tied to one's connection with a particular local body of believers. Therefore it would prove irregular to receive baptism separately from a local church body and an ordained minister of the gospel. Irregular, however, does not equal invalid—and in fact necessity may dictate irregularity (e.g., in a missions context somewhere that local churches may not be established, in a place where the church is persecuted, and so on).[21] But irregularity should be avoided if possible.

What if the person who baptized me later denied the faith?

Again, the efficacy of baptism is not tied to the person who administers it. It would be an awful thing if that were true—we would need to maintain a watchful eye, for the rest of our days, on the person who administered our baptism, and doubt would always remain about whether our baptism would prove, in the end, to be a true baptism. But this is not the case. The Spirit's working and Christ's blessing, according to the covenant promises of God the Father, make baptism effectual. It is dependent on him—not someone else.

Should I leave a church that practices baptism differently from the way I believe?

Not necessarily. When congregants of the church

that I serve are moving to a new area, I tell them, "Find a Bible-believing church that preaches the Word faithfully and where elders shepherd the flock and you can serve." If you belong to a church like this, thank God. It is a good and rare church—don't dismiss the great by instead seeking the ideal. You should seriously weigh the option of staying and serving, without being combative over this doctrine, if you are able. It may, however, be necessary or even beneficial for you (and for that church) to instead find a church that practices baptism in a way that is closer to your convictions about it. This decision should be made with the counsel of your current pastor and elders. If you have taken vows of membership at that church, your loyalty lies there until the Lord makes it clear that you should move on. And if you do so, I pray it is with tears and not a haughty spirit.

I am convinced about covenantal baptism, but I am a member of a baptistic church, and my children can't receive the sacrament here. Is this a reason to leave?

Probably; but again, I would weigh this decision heavily. Your children are not somehow "lesser" covenant children if they are raised in a baptistic church. Though my baptistic friends don't realize that all the children in their churches are members of the covenant community, their personal conviction doesn't nullify the fact that this is indeed true. Your children are still covenant children, even though they are missing some of the blessings of inclusion in that covenant. I would pray, talk with advisors, and consult with your current pastor(s) and elders. It may be that you will indeed have to move your membership—but you will want to do so with conviction (and a measure of sorrow).

If I have family members who don't believe in covenantal baptism, should I invite them to the service in which our child is baptized?

Absolutely. Invite them, with the knowledge that they will view the service differently. I married into a wonderfully strong baptistic family. When I baptized my daughter, we invited all my in-laws to attend. The entire weekend was filled with comments like "I'm looking forward to the baby dedication"; "What a nice baby dedication"; "Congratulations on dedicating your baby." It was fine, and we were blessed to have them there. I was happy for them to witness a covenantal baptism and to hear it explained—especially since I was the one performing and explaining it!

Should I marry someone with whom I disagree regarding baptism?

I encourage couples to sort through this issue before marriage. It seldom becomes easier for them to do so later, and when they conceive their first child, the pressure surrounding this issue heightens—which raises the bar of stress in a young marriage. Can it work? Of course.

Can it be sorted out later? Yes. But is it better to agree before vows are exchanged? Absolutely.

My spouse and I disagree on whether to baptize our children. What should we do?

First, be patient and gracious with each other. Spend concerted times of prayer and study together. I would suggest reading some of the recommended resources at the end of this book. Choose one or two of them to read together. Then find a book that cogently presents a baptistic view and read it together. Search the Scriptures. Trust each other enough to actually engage in dialogue about this, ask each other questions, and share your concerns. I would take time to go through this process. But in the event that you spend a lot of time and energy doing so without reaching an agreement, I would encourage the husband to seek counsel from his pastor and elders. He will then need to make a decision about it—hopefully after hearing the counsel and receiving the support of his wife.

Must a person be baptized before being admitted to the Lord's Table?

Yes—baptism is the sacrament of initiation into the covenant people of God. This is why it occurs once and why it occurs before communion can be taken. Meanwhile, the Lord's Table is observed regularly throughout the course of a Christian's life instead of simply once. It serves as the sacrament of spiritual nourishment and is to be taken primarily with the local body to which a Christian has committed himself or herself by taking its membership vows.

I attend a baptistic church, and they want me to be "rebaptized" before I can come to the Table. Should I do so?

If you are convinced of the truth that the baptism you received as an infant or a child was a true baptism, then you should not participate in what they are requiring. It would go against your conscience to participate in it—and it is not good to go against one's conscience. This most likely means that you will need to begin searching for a new church. Not being a member of the church you attend or being able to come to the Table with your brothers and sisters in Christ can be endured for a season, but doing so is deleterious over a long period of time.

Do you have to believe in covenantal baptism in order to serve as an officer in a Reformed or Presbyterian church?

Most Reformed or Presbyterian churches require their officers to hold to a covenantal view of baptism. This is because churches in this tradition usually require their officers to subscribe to confessional standards (e.g., the Westminster Standards, Three Forms of Unity, and so on). This requirement helps to safeguard the teaching, unity, and faithfulness of the church. A person's view on covenantal baptism affects many different areas of that person's doctrine, and not subscribing to it would also mean not subscribing to most Reformed or Presbyterian confessions. This does not, however, mean that an individual with baptistic convictions cannot occupy other leadership positions in such a church. Some of the most servant-hearted leaders in different areas of the church that I serve hold baptistic convictions, and they are well respected; our church would suffer without them. They just can't be officers.

Is baptism made too much of in the church today? There seems to be a lot of disagreement and division over who receives it and how it is performed. Is it worth all this?

It is certainly possible to make too much of baptism—but we also risk making too little of it. The discussions about it are worth having—but always in love. Truth matters, and so we honor the Lord when we attempt to ascertain and maintain what the Scriptures teach. There is a loving and gracious way of doing this, however. I for one am always happy—well, *usually* happy—when people want to discuss baptism. It affords me the opportunity to discuss the kindness of our covenant-keeping, sinner-saving, truth-defining, sovereign God. That is a good thing. And we can have these discussions well, and to the glory of the Father, by abiding in the grace of Christ and the fellowship of the Spirit.

RECOMMENDED RESOURCES

Additional Books on Baptism

Chaney, James M. *William the Baptist: A Classic Story of a Man's Journey to Understand Baptism*. Updated by Ronald Evans. Phillipsburg, NJ: P&R Publishing, 2011. [This book, adapted from a work that was first published in the 1870s, is delightfully written. Chaney provides a running dialogue between a Baptist named William and a Presbyterian pastor. Their conversation covers a wide range of concerns that people with a baptistic view often have regarding covenantal baptism and provides helpful and stirring responses.]

Fesko, J. V. Word, *Water, and Spirit: A Reformed Perspective on Baptism*. Grand Rapids: Reformation Heritage Books, 2010. [In my opinion, Fesko's work provides the most comprehensive and detailed explanation of baptism that is available today. This resource will prove beneficial for those who desire an in-depth exploration of this doctrine.]

Murray, John. *Christian Baptism*. Reprint, Phillipsburg, NJ: Presbyterian and Reformed Publishing Company, 1980. [Dr. Murray wrote a modern-day classic on the doctrine of baptism. He understood how to use an economy of words without neglecting essentials, making this a brief yet helpful read.]

Richard, Guy M. *Baptism: Answers to Common Questions*. Orlando: Reformation Trust Publishing, 2019. [This recent publication helpfully interacts with contemporary baptistic questions and concerns. It is easily accessible and readable.]

Ward, Rowland S. *Baptism in Scripture and History: A Fresh Study of the Meaning and Mode of Christian Baptism*. Victoria, Australia: Globe Press, 1991. [Ward provides a helpful, short read that is evenly divided between baptism in Scripture and baptism in history.]

Books on Covenant Theology

Rhodes, Jonty. *Covenants Made Simple: Understanding God's Unfolding Promises to His People*. Phillipsburg, NJ: P&R Publishing, 2014. [The title says it all. If you are looking for an introduction to the basics of covenant theology, you won't find a better resource than this. The structure, flow, and readability of this book could not be better. It makes for an easy entry point for understanding covenant theology.]

Robertson, O. Palmer. *The Christ of the Covenants*. Phillipsburg, NJ: Presbyterian and Reformed Publishing Company, 1980. [From a Reformed perspective, this is one of the most important books that was published in the late twentieth century. Through it, Dr. Robertson stirred a generation of Presbyterian students and pastors to a greater understanding of the way God has worked in salvation history through the covenants.]

Books on Raising Covenant Children

Beeke, Joel R. *Bringing the Gospel to Covenant Children*. Grand Rapids: Reformation Heritage Books, 2010. [This very small book provides parents with practical guidance on how to share the faith with their covenant children. It showcases Dr. Beeke's natural warmth and heart for Christ.]

Helopoulos, Jason. *Let the Children Worship*. Fearn, Ross-shire, UK: Christian Focus Publications, 2016. [This book encourages readers to include children in the church's corporate worship services and presents the biblical and theological framework for doing so—as well as the practical benefits. In addition, it provides suggestions and helps for parents, pastors, and congregations who are embarking upon this delight.]

———. *A Neglected Grace: Family Worship in the Christian Home.* Reprint, Fearn, Ross-shire, UK: Christian Focus Publications, 2013. [Nothing will benefit your family more than a regular habit of family worship. In this book, I provide encouragements and practical suggestions for enjoying this life-giving practice in your family.]

A CLOSING PRAYER FOR OUR COVENANT CHILDREN

Give them sorrows, but not too deep;
struggles, but not too great.
Make them seasoned, but not hopeless;
comfortable in their own skin, but not vain;
zealous, but equally wise;
knowledgeable, but filled with humility;
content, but continually striving.
Allow them to be confident, but not cocky;
humble, but not sheepish;
gracious, but not fearful.
Mature their bodies with strength,
their emotions with sophistication,
and their imaginations with brilliance.
Fill their lungs with deep laughter
and their souls with joy.

Yet, even as I pray these things,
there is one prayer that soars above the rest:

Bestow upon them your grace.
Lavish them with your mercy.
Drench them with your love.
Fill them with your Holy Spirit.
Bless them with a glimpse of your glory,
that their affections may rise.
Give them the gift of faith.
Satiate all their appetites with you.
Set them apart for your holy service.
Bring them into living union with your Son.
Grant that my children would be your children.
May all that was signified in their baptisms be sealed
        to them.
What glory that would give to your name,
and what joy it would give to my heart.
Be gracious, my covenant-keeping God.

I pray all this in faith, remembering your covenant
        pledge:
"This promise is for you and for your children."

Amen.

NOTES

Foreword

1 David E. Garland, *1 Corinthians*, Baker Exegetical Commentary on the New Testament (Grand Rapids: Baker Academic, 2003), 674.

Introduction: Beginning with the Right Perspective

1 "Catholic" in this context refers to the universal church, not the Roman Catholic church. This is the historical meaning of the word—as is seen in the Apostle's Creed.

2 Meaning one who believes in infant baptism.

3 Quoted in William Knight, *Colloquia Peripatetica: Deep-Sea Soundings; Being Notes of Conversations with the Late John Duncan*, 5th ed. (Edinburgh, 1879), 8.

4 I will use this term throughout the book to refer to the baptizing of children. Others may call this practice infant baptism or paedobaptism, and those are fine names for it. But since our covenantal theology forms the basis of the view of baptism that leads Reformed churches to baptize the children of their communing members, the term *covenantal baptism* best represents this view.

5 I will refer to this view, throughout the book, as a "baptistic" view of baptism. And, of course, there are other terms employed for *this* view as well—some prefer credobaptism, believer's baptism, believers-only baptism, and so on; but for the sake of simplicity I will refer to it as the "baptist" or "baptistic" view.

Chapter 1: The Kindness of God

1   O. Palmer Robertson, *The Christ of the Covenants* (Phillipsburg, NJ: Presbyterian and Reformed Publishing, 1980), 4.

2   Jonty Rhodes, *Covenants Made Simple: Understanding God's Unfolding Promises to His People* (repr., Phillipsburg, NJ: P&R Publishing, 2014), 18.

3   Some Reformed theologians have maintained that a tricovenantal (three-covenant) system exists—one that includes a separate covenant of redemption between the persons of the triune Godhead. Shedd comments on this by saying, "Though this distinction [between the covenant of redemption and the covenant of grace] is favored by the Scripture statements, it does not follow that there are two separate and independent covenants antithetic to the covenant of works. The covenant of grace and that of redemption are two modes or phases of the one evangelical covenant of mercy." William G. T. Shedd, *Dogmatic Theology* (New York, 1888), 2:360.

4   William Hendriksen in *The Covenant of Grace* (Grand Rapids: Baker Book House, 1932), 12, provides the following passages as a sampling: Genesis 15:18; 17:2–21; 26:23–25; 28:13–15; Ex. 6:2–8; 19:1–6; 24:7–8; Lev. 26:14ff., 23–24, 40–45; Deut. 4:23–31; Josh. 23:16; Judg. 2:20–22; 2 Sam. 23:5; 1 Kings 8:23; 19:10; 2 Kings 13:23; 17:15–18, 34–41; 23:3; 1 Chron. 16:15ff.; 2 Chron. 5:10; 21:7; Ps. 25:14; 74:20; 89:28; 103:17–18; 105:8–10; 111:5; 132:12; Jer. 31:31–34; Dan. 9:4ff.; Luke 1:54–55, 72–73; 22:20; Acts 2:38–39; Rom. 11:27; Gal. 3:9, 17, 29; Heb. 8:6ff.; 10:16, 29; 12:24; 13:20.

5   John Murray, *Christian Baptism* (Phillipsburg, NJ: Presbyterian and Reformed Publishing, 1980), 47.

6   Genesis 12:1–3; 13:14–16; 15:18–21; 17:1–16; 22:16–18.

7   Robert L. Reymond, *A New Systematic Theology of the Christian Faith* (Nashville: Thomas Nelson Publishers, 1998), 513.

8   At this point in Genesis, Abraham still bears the name Abram. However, for simplicity's sake, I'm using his fuller name here.

9   See Augustine, on John 6:41–49, in tractate 26.11 of "Homilies on the Gospel of John," trans. John Gibb and James Innes, in *A Select*

Library of the Nicene and Post-Nicene Fathers of the Christian Church, 1st ser., ed. Philip Schaff, vol. 7, *St. Augustin: Homilies on the Gospel of John, Homilies on the First Epistle of John, Soliloquies* (New York, 1888), 171; as well as Augustine, on 1 John 3:19–4:3, in homily 6.11 of "Homilies on the First Epistle of John," trans. H. Browne, rev. and ed. Joseph H. Myers, in *Nicene and Post-Nicene Fathers,* 498–99.

10 *Calvin: Institutes of the Christian Religion,* ed. John T. McNeill, trans. Ford Lewis Battles, vol. 2, *Books III.XX to IV.XX* (Philadelphia: Westminster Press, 1960), 4.14.3.

11 See Murray, *Christian Baptism,* for a full defense of this argument, 45–48.

12 Westminster Shorter Catechism, answer 16.

13 Herman Bavinck, *Reformed Dogmatics,* ed. John Bolt, trans. John Vriend, vol. 4, *Holy Spirit, Church, and New Creation* (Grand Rapids: Baker Academic, 2008), 476.

14 See Sinclair B. Ferguson, "Infant Baptism View," in *Baptism: Three Views,* ed. David F. Wright (Downers Grove: IVP Academic, 2009), 93.

Chapter 2: The Fourfold Stream of Testimony

1 Ulrich Zwingli, the sixteenth-century leader of the Reformation in Switzerland, is a prime example. He turned the Anabaptists—a radical element of the Reformation who advocated for believer's baptism only and were debating with him—to the covenant for proof of the doctrine of infant baptism. See Robert L. Reymond, *A New Systematic Theology of the Christian Faith* (Nashville: Thomas Nelson Publishers, 1998), 503.

2 Of course, discontinuity also exists. The move from the old covenant to the new covenant involved changes (in the areas of the sacraments, the sacrificial system, the ceremonial law, and so on). Everyone recognizes that there is both discontinuity and continuity. However, whereas dispensationalism maintains that discontinuity is central to biblical interpretation, Reformed Theology has primarily seen continuity between the old covenant and the new covenant.

3 Joel R. Beeke and Ray B. Lanning, "Unto You, and to Your

Children," in *The Case for Covenantal Infant Baptism*, ed. Gregg Strawbridge (Phillipsburg, NJ: P&R Publishing, 2003), 58.

4   Geoffrey Bromiley, *The Baptism of Infants* (London: Church Book Room Press, 1955), 12.

5   *Calvin: Institutes of the Christian Religion*, ed. John T. McNeill, trans. Ford Lewis Battles, vol. 2, *Books III.XX to IV.XX* (Philadelphia: Westminster Press, 1960), 4.16.11.

6   John Murray, *Christian Baptism* (Phillipsburg, NJ: Presbyterian and Reformed Publishing, 1980), 64.

7   Reymond, *A New Systematic Theology*, 941.

8   See Acts 2:41; 8:12, 13, 38; 9:18; 10:48; 16:15, 33; 18:8; 19:5; 1 Corinthians 1:14, 16.

9   Geoffrey W. Bromiley, "The Meaning and Scope of Baptism," in *Major Themes in the Reformed Tradition*, ed. Donald K. McKim (Grand Rapids: William B. Eerdmans, 1992), 238.

10 Although Tertullian mentioned it in the context of opposing it. Joachim Jeremias's work, *Infant Baptism in the First Four Centuries*, trans. David Cairns (1960; repr., Eugene, OR: Wipf & Stock, 2004) continues to be a helpful resource on this topic.

11 Origen, *Homilies on Leviticus: 1–16*, trans. Gary Wayne Barkley, The Fathers of the Church 83 (Washington, D. C.: The Catholic University of America Press, 1990), 8.3.5.

12 See Augustine, bk. 4, chap. 24.32, of "On Baptism, against the Donatists," trans. J. R. King, in *A Select Library of the Nicene and Post-Nicene Fathers of the Christian Church*, 1st ser., ed. Philip Schaff, vol. 4, *St. Augustin: The Writings against the Manichaeans, and against the Donatists* (Buffalo, 1887), 461–62.

13 See Louis Igou Hodges, *Reformed Theology Today* (Columbus, GA: Brentwood Christian Press, 1995), 122, who cites this point to "Augustine, Anti-Donatist works, 4.100.15."

Chapter 3: Blessings to the Children

1   Some of these thoughts were first communicated in Jason Helopoulos, *Let the Children Worship* (Fearn, Ross-shire, UK: Christian Focus Publications, 2016).

2 See Edmund P. Clowney, *The Church*, Contours of Christian Theology (Downers Grove: InterVarsity Press, 1995), 278.

3 Sinclair B. Ferguson, "Infant Baptism View," in *Baptism: Three Views*, ed. David F. Wright (Downers Grove: IVP Academic, 2009), 90.

4 J. Ligon Duncan III, "The Abrahamic Covenant: Covenant Signs; Covenant Sign Implications," Reformed Perspectives Magazine 15, no. 3 (August 11–17 2013), available online at https://thirdmill .org/articles/jl_duncan/jl_duncan.CT006.html, emphasis added.

5 *Calvin: Institutes of the Christian Religion*, ed. John T. McNeill, trans. Ford Lewis Battles, vol. 2, *Books III.XX to IV.XX* (Philadelphia: Westminster Press, 1960), 4.14.9.

6 Answer 92, emphasis added.

7 The literal meaning of this expression is "from the work performed," and it takes the view that grace is always conferred by a sacrament itself, by virtue of the rite being performed.

8 J. V. Fesko, *Word, Water, and Spirit: A Reformed Perspective on Baptism* (Grand Rapids: Reformation Heritage Books, 2010), 282, emphasis added.

9 See Calvin, *Institutes*, 4.14.17.

10 John Murray, *Christian Baptism* (Phillipsburg, NJ: Presbyterian and Reformed Publishing, 1980), 86.

11 Murray, 86.

12 Geoffrey W. Bromiley, *Children of Promise: The Case for Baptizing Infants* (repr., Eugene, OR: Wipf & Stock, 1998), 81.

13 Robert Letham, *Systematic Theology* (Wheaton, IL: Crossway, 2019), 645.

14 See the Westminster Larger Catechism, answer 162.

15 Fesko, *Word, Water, and Spirit*, 326.

16 No. 6830 of *D. Martin Luthers Tischreden: 1531–46*, vol. 6, *Tischreden aus verschiedenen Jahren*, D. Martin Luthers Werke: Kritische Gesammtausgabe (Weimar, Germany: Hermann Böhlaus Nachfolger, 1921), 217, quoted in Heiko A. Oberman, *Luther: Man between God and the Devil*, trans. Eileen Walliser-Schwarzbart (repr., New Haven: Yale University Press, 2006), 105.

Chapter 4: Blessings to the Parents

1   *The Book of Church Order of the Presbyterian Church in America* (Lawrenceville, GA: The Office of the Stated Clerk of the General Assembly of the Presbyterian Church of America, 2019), 56-5.

2   Another way of saying this is that we approach our own souls as grace-saturated Calvinists but approach our children's souls as, at best, Arminians and, at worst, works-saturated semi-Pelagians.

3   Dane Ortlund, *Gentle and Lowly: The Heart of Christ for Sinners and Suffering* (Wheaton, IL: Crossway, 2020), 100.

4   Samuel Miller, *Infant Baptism Scriptural and Reasonable: and Baptism by Sprinkling or Affusion, the Most Suitable and Edifying Mode; in Four Discourses* (Philadelphia, 1835), 65.

5   I have written a book on this subject that provides help and encouragement: Jason Helopoulos, *A Neglected Grace: Family Worship in the Christian Home* (Fearn, Ross-shire, UK: Christian Focus Publications, 2013).

6   Additional information can be found in a book that I published on this subject: Jason Helopoulos, Let the Children Worship (Fearn, Ross-shire, UK: Christian Focus), 2016. It provides both the biblical and theological arguments in favor of including children in corporate worship as well as practical help regarding how to do so.

7   Charles Hodge, "Bushnell on Christian Nurture," *Biblical Repertory and Princeton Review* 19, no. 4 (October 1847): 507. reprinted in Charles Hodge, *Essays and Reviews* (New York, 1857), 309.

Chapter 5: Blessings to the Congregation

1   *The Book of Church Order of the Presbyterian Church in America* (Lawrenceville, GA: The Office of the Stated Clerk of the General Assembly of the Presbyterian Church of America, 2019), 56–5.

2   Bryan Chapell, "A Pastoral Overview of Infant Baptism," in *The Case for Covenantal Infant Baptism*, ed. Gregg Strawbridge (Phillipsburg, NJ: P&R Publishing, 2003), 26.

3   We do, however, need to be careful—and especially today— to make sure that children are interacting with adults in a safe church environment. Deepak Reju's book, *On Guard: Preventing*

and Responding to Child Abuse at Church (Greensboro, NC: New Growth Press, 2014), serves as a helpful tool for doing so.

4 J. V. Fesko, *Word, Water, and Spirit: A Reformed Perspective on Baptism* (Grand Rapids: Reformation Heritage Books, 2010), 320.

5 John Murray, *Christian Baptism* (Phillipsburg, NJ: Presbyterian and Reformed Publishing, 1980), 3.

6 Sinclair B. Ferguson, "Infant Baptism View," in *Baptism: Three Views*, ed. David F. Wright (Downers Grove: IVP Academic, 2009), 110.

Questions and Answers on Baptism

1 R.C. Sproul, *What Is Baptism* (Orlando: Reformation Trust Publishing, 2011), 19.

2 Sinclair B. Ferguson, "Infant Baptism View," in *Baptism: Three Views*, ed. David F. Wright (Downers Grove: IVP Academic, 2009), 89.

3 B. B. Warfield, "The Polemics of Infant Baptism," *The Presbyterian Quarterly*, no. 48 (April 1899): 314.

4 Warfield, 314.

5 Johannes Cocceius, *Explicatio Catecheseos Heidelbergensis*, in *Opera Omnia Theologica, Exegetica, Didactica, Polemica, Philologica*, vol. 7 (repr., Amsterdam, 1701), quoted in Herman Witsius, "On the Efficacy and Utility of Baptism in the Case of Elect Infants Whose Parents Are Under the Covenant," trans. William Marshall, ed. and rev. trans. J. Mark Beach, *Mid-America Journal of Theology* 17 (2006): 129, available online at https://www.midamerica.edu/uploads /files/pdf/journal/17-witsius.pdf.

6 Cocceius, quoted in Witsius.

7 Louis Berkhof, *Systematic Theology*, new combined ed. (Grand Rapids: Wm. B. Eerdmans, 1996), 618–19.

8 Geoffrey W. Bromiley, *Children of Promise: The Case for Baptizing Infants* (repr., Eugene, OR: Wipf & Stock, 1998), 21.

9 J. V. Fesko, *Word, Water, and Spirit: A Reformed Perspective on Baptism* (Grand Rapids: Reformation Heritage Books, 2010), 356.

10 See Rowland S. Ward, *Baptism in Scripture and History: A Fresh Study of the Meaning and Mode of Christian Baptism* (Victoria, Australia: Globe Press, 1991), 53.

11 As the Westminster Confession of Faith states, "Dipping of the person into the water is not necessary; but baptism is rightly administered by pouring or sprinkling water upon the person" (28.3).

12 John Murray, *Christian Baptism* (Phillipsburg, NJ: Presbyterian and Reformed Publishing, 1980), 23–24.

13 Josephus, *History of the Jewish War against the Romans*, trans. Henry St. John Thackeray, bk. 4.3.3, quoted in Leon Morris, *The Epistle to the Romans*, The Pillar New Testament Commentary Series (Grand Rapids: Wm. B. Eerdmans, 1988), 246.

14 See question 161 of the Westminster Larger Catechism and question 91 of the Westminster Shorter Catechism.

15 *Calvin: Institutes of the Christian Religion*, ed. John T. McNeill, trans. Ford Lewis Battles, vol. 2, *Books III.XX to IV.XX* (Philadelphia: Westminster Press, 1960), 4.14.17.

16 See Dr. Ligon Duncan's helpful explanation at "Is There an Age of Accountability?" Reformed Theological Seminary, May 5, 2020, https://rts.edu/resources/is-there-an-age-of-accountability/.

17 Fesko, *Word, Water, and Spirit*, 355.

18 Fesko, 356.

19 "Romish Baptism" in "Art. IV: The General Assembly," *The Princeton Review* 17, no. 3 (July 1845): 452, reprinted in Charles Hodge, *Discussions in Church Polity* (New York, 1878), 198.

20 See the Westminster Larger Catechism, answer 161.

21 The Reformed Church in America serves as another example. Back when the RCA initially spread to the western frontier of the growing United States, the insufficient number of ordained pastors in the area led to the decision that ruling elders should also administer the sacraments.

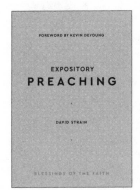

"David Strain has given us a thoughtful, engaging, stimulating primer on the importance of hearing God's Word. . . . Strain understands how vital it is for church members to hear God's Word rightly and have it shape how they think and live. . . . A must-read for church members and pastors alike."
—**Ian Hamilton**, Professor of Systematic and Historical Theology, Greenville Presbyterian Theological Seminary

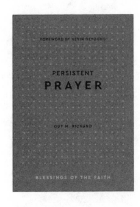

"I love this book! In an inviting and compelling way, *Persistent Prayer* captures the desperate, urgent need we have to pray. . . . You will find yourself encouraged and inspired to talk to God. Thank you, Guy, for giving us such clear answers, anchored in the Scriptures, for why we should pray. What a gift."
—**Crawford W. Loritts Jr.**, Author; Speaker; Radio Host